How to Make It to Friday

Larry Jones

Foreword by
Gene Garrison

Harvest House Publishers
Irvine, California 92714

HOW TO MAKE IT TO FRIDAY

Copyright © 1980 by Harvest House Publishers
Irvine, California 92714

Library of Congress Catalog Card Number 79-67429
ISBN: 0-89081-210-1

Printed in the United States of America.

Foreword

One of the common criticisms of evangelism is that it often neglects or overlooks the life-centered needs of people who are already saved. This is a justifiable complaint against certain evangelists who are intent on telling people how to become Christians, but fail to tell them how to live like Christians. How does a believer handle worry . . . fear . . . tension . . . and the multitude of pressing problems of everyday living?

Larry Jones has not forgotten this dimension of evangelism! His ministry not only directs people into the Kingdom through the grace of God, but also offers down-to-earth help in appropriating that same grace in facing the difficulties and frustrations of life. *How to Make It to Friday* is a book pointing in that direction—intensely practical and helpful for all Christians, from the newborn babe in Christ to the most mature disciple. It should be well-received by every member of the family of God.

It is my privilege to serve as pastor to the Larry Jones family—and to be their friend as well. Thus I have had opportunity to observe the entire family applying the principles in this book to their own lives. Larry Jones speaks and writes out of a compassionate heart and with a background of personal spiritual growth.

I highly recommend the book for the help it will bring to everyone who reads it and takes its message seriously.

—Gene Garrison

Acknowledgements

A special thanks goes to Dr. C.A. Roberts. He taught me that a book is sometimes louder than words . . . that a novel can grip the heart and convey the message of truth . . . and that there is sometimes a beginning before the beginning. I regret that he was taken in a car accident before this project was completed.

The beginning of a book usually starts without a pen. Then that moment comes to speak with the written word. All of life seems to go through that pen. Therefore, it is impossible to take credit for a book. Experiences, remembered and forgotten, are a part of every person. A lifetime is engulfed in these pages.

Even though this is a novel, it is interwoven with truth. Thanks go to my wife for helping to write a book with her life. She has influenced me directly and indirectly.

A word of gratitude goes to those thousands who have shared their problems and hurts over the past fifteen years. Their lives have become a part of me. Much of this book grew out of sharing and writing about the answers found in Christ. As you continue in your struggles, may the ray of hope in Christ give light to your path.

—Larry Jones

Contents

Introduction

❖

Sunday, 10:00 p.m.

When did weekends start getting lost? How did they go from full to empty without something in between? How does the mere absence of kids, who were in their own world anyway, create such a void? When did cigarettes and liquor start keeping me awake and not putting me to sleep?

She was sitting in her "drinking chair," as she had come to call it. Excepting two trips to the bathroom, she had not moved for hours. The ice had melted in her glass, and the open bottle of vodka stood close by on the nightstand. She had made no pretense of mixing a martini, or even getting an olive for the last two drinks; just straight vodka over ice.

What happens to time? It's dragging and rushing me. I waited all week for Friday. Now the weekend is gone, but where did it go? When did Paul say he would be home? Was it Tuesday, or Thursday? Seems like it was a day that started with a "t." How long has he been gone? A week? No, two weeks. Last weekend was lost, too. Why haven't the kids called? Oh, God! The phone rang last night, and I didn't answer it . . . or did I? No. I would have remembered. Surely.

The television set kept the silence broken, as it had done through the day. Church services, basketball games, racing cars, detective shows, and movies. Although she had not bothered to be selective, she had tried to listen, at times making a conscious effort to see how long she could keep her mind on the program. No luck. Couldn't concentrate. Occasionally, welcome sleep broke in, but never for long.

Regardless of momentary outside distractions, her mind always drifted back toward the same thing . . . that big, thick, suffocating sense of emptiness. Absolute, total emptiness. Like a deep, black hole in the center of her mind. At times she told herself she was going crazy. Unfortunately, she knew that wasn't the case. That would be too simple.

WHAT am I going to do? What am I GOING to do? What am I going to DO? . . . to do . . . to do . . . when I'm twice as old as I am now, I'll be ninety-two years old. My oldest will be older than I am now. Ninety-two . . . who lives to ninety-two? Who cares? Friday — that's the trick. You just have to keep getting to Friday.

She reached for the phone as she had a dozen times in the last two hours. Twice she had dialed the number . . . once even waited for someone to answer. Having no pen within reach, she had memorized the number earlier in the day after hearing it on television. She was proud of her accomplishment, but it hadn't been easy. From the moment the number had flashed on the screen, she had scrambled for association — 528-8300. *In eight years, Paul would be fifty-two. In eight years, I'll still have three children. Oh, oh!*

She dialed the number again. It was either get ice, go to the bathroom or talk. The alternatives had been going through her mind when the ten o'clock news prompted a decision. She had better do it while she could still speak without slurring her words.

Three rings . . . four . . . this is Sunday night. What am I thinking? Preachers aren't home. They're in church . . . five . . . but he wasn't in church this morning. He was on television . . . six . . . that's enough . . . .

"Hello."

He's there.

"Hello."

"Oh, excuse me. Is Reverend Jones in?"

"This is he."

"Please forgive me for calling at this hour, but you gave your number on TV this morning, and I . . . well, I didn't really think you would be home . . . on Sunday evening, you know."

"I'm not at home. You reached me at my office."

"Oh, I see. I should have known . . . you probably wouldn't give your home number . . . but I'm glad you do this . . . take calls from old ladies, I mean."

"Normally, I don't, at least not on Sunday night. There are others who usually take the calls. I came by for some papers and saw the light blinking on my phone. I can't ignore a ringing telephone, so I picked it up. May I ask who is calling?"

"I'm sorry, I should have told you. My name is Amy . . . Amy Wortham. I live here . . . in Oklahoma City. I saw you on television this morning. Not the first time . . . you gave your address, and said if we had an urgent need to call. Well, I don't know if my situation is urgent, but I never would have written, and I just had to talk to someone — at least I thought I did.''

"You don't have to explain, is it Mrs. Wortham?''

"Yes.''

"How can I help?''

Now what do I say? Why did I call? How can I explain what I don't understand myself? He's waiting for me to answer. I've got to say something . . . anything . . . .

"Reverend Jones, I feel very foolish, and I detest people who play on the dramatic . . . but I . . . I think I . . . really need . . . help.''

Why doesn't he answer? What else can I say? This is the first time I've admitted even to myself that I need help. What else is there to say? I can't do this . . . at least, not on the phone! How do I get out of this?

"Reverend Jones, I know it's late, and I don't know what to say . . . would it be possible to make an appointment to see you? Do you ever do that sort of thing?''

"Not as much as I would like, Mrs. Wortham, because my schedule keeps me on the move. However, when I'm in town, I try to see as many people as I can. It so happens I'll be home this next week. Let's see, I don't have my calendar with me, but I'm sure I'll have some time later in the week. How would next Friday morning about eleven o'clock suit you?''

Friday? Dear God, how can he ask me to wait 'til Friday? That's the whole problem . . . Friday . . . how can I make it to Friday?

"Mrs. Wortham? How about next Friday?''

"You see, that's what I wanted to talk to you about."

"I don't think I understand."

"Friday . . ." she paused again. Was she crying? No. "Here I go with the dramatics again . . . ." Now she was crying.

"Mrs. Wortham . . . ."

"I'm sorry . . . I didn't mean to do that . . . what I meant was . . . Reverend Jones, how does one make it to Friday? Not next Friday . . . any Friday. I know how to get through the weekend—I have it beside me here on the table. But I'm running out of ways to make it through the big stretch . . . . Look, Reverend Jones, forgive me for bothering you. I have the feeling I should be able to give you a one sentence statement of my problem, and I can't do it. I couldn't if I had a week. All I know is that all weekend I've had this thing in the back of my mind telling me I wasn't going to make it. I've been trying to ignore it—trying hard. But when you said the word Friday—well . . . ."

The tears were coming again, and she couldn't shut them off. Amy felt her eyes stinging . . . heard her voice blurting out the tumbling, hurried words—"I just don't think I'm going to make it to one more Friday! And if I do, there will just be one more lost weekend and one more journey to another Friday . . . and another . . . oh, God, I wish . . . ."

"Can you make it to nine o'clock in the morning? If so, meet me at my office—same address as on television."

"Reverend Jones, I didn't mean to be pushy, and I don't want to impose. But when I heard you this morning, it was like . . . ."

"Mrs. Wortham, if we are going to make it to Friday, we need an early start. Let's just say nine a.m. sharp. Okay?"

"Okay. And . . . Reverend Jones?"

"Yes."

". . . thanks."

"Goodnight."

"Goodnight."

As Amy placed the phone on the receiver, she turned out the light and leaned back, staring into the dark. *Oh, God, let me make it to one more Friday—and if I do, let it be a different kind of Friday.*

How to Focus Your Sorrow

1

Monday, 9:00 A.M.

She was younger than I imagined her from our phone conversation. Somehow the quality of her voice, the weariness I had detected the night before, had created an impression of age, and I had subconsciously envisioned an older person. Mrs. Amy Wortham did not look to be more than forty.

Despite her efforts to look her best for the occasion, there was a line here, a shadow beneath the eyes, a barely perceptible coarseness, none of which was necessarily permanent. It simply could have been the aftermath of a hard weekend.

We exchanged greetings and quickly drifted toward a prolonged, almost awkward silence. Amy sat looking at her hands on her lap. She appeared reluctant to speak for fear of crying. After a long moment, she drew a deep breath, as though she needed strength to speak.

"Mrs. Wortham, where would you like to begin?"

Amy did not look up at first. When she began speaking, it was hardly above a whisper.

"Reverend Jones, you may be looking at the most mixed-up, fouled-up woman you have met in a long while. Where to begin . . . I almost feel like the magician who says, 'Take a card.' "

I waited for her to go on.

Looking up, she continued, "I am sad. I'm lonely. I'm afraid. I worry and have doubts. I have guilts. I get depressed, discouraged and . . . I know all this sounds silly, but every time I read where someone is talking about their problems I find myself saying, 'That's me.' I feel like my life has become a pot with no handle . . . there simply doesn't seem to be any way to get ahold of myself.

"Sometimes I feel like a car we used to have. We were so proud of it when it was new. We worried about every little scratch or every little squeak. But as the years went by, we took less care of it. We went longer without getting it repaired. Finally, the day came when my husband said it would be cheaper to get a new car than to fix the old one. Too many things were wrong. That's how I feel about my life. The problem is . . . there isn't any way to trade me in on a new model."

Amy waited to let her words sink in. Her last statement was more of a challenge to me than an opinion that she felt strongly.

I knew exactly where she was. For most people, the distance between everything being fine and everything being wrong is not far. All the difficulties she had mentioned would have to be dealt with one by one. Discouragement, despair, disappointment, depression, sorrow, guilt, fear — all of these were very real problems in her life. It also was obvious to me that certain basic chords in her spirit were out of tune, making her vulnerable.

"All I can say, Mrs. Wortham, is thank God it's Monday."

"Thank God it's Monday? I'm afraid you have missed me."

"Well, if I were an automobile mechanic and you brought your car to me and described as many things wrong with it as you just did about yourself, I would have fainted if you had asked to have your car that afternoon. Actually, Mrs. Wortham, I was referring to our conversation last night when we talked about helping you make it to Friday. With as many problems as you have mentioned, we'll need all week."

A deeper frown worked its way across her brow.

"Have you had much success at things like this, Reverend Jones . . . I mean working with people like me?"

I leaned across and took my Bible from the corner of the desk and held it out, looking into her eyes.

"Mrs. Wortham, I'm not a psychiatrist. However, I serve One who has been called the Great Physician, and I have never seen His prescriptions fail. I'm not about to make light of your troubles, but I don't believe there is a problem that you and I and the Lord, all working together, can't solve."

She took a handkerchief from her purse as though anticipating her need for it.

Amy's voice quivered, "I guess that brings us back to the question you asked, 'Where do we begin?' "

"Let me make a suggestion, Mrs. Wortham. Let's begin with the most immediate need pressing on your mind. If you could have one of your problems solved first, which would it be? What has been most on your mind recently? Let's assume we could solve all your problems in time, but some take three months, some two months, some one month, some two weeks. What is it, this very moment, which concerns you most?''

When Amy began, it was as if she were trying to talk through her handkerchief, holding it partially across her mouth. Now and then she would pause, fighting back tears.

''There is something I did not mention to you. I was afraid to bring it up because immediately you would think that one thing was causing all my other problems. But that isn't true! My mother died two months ago. We were very close and we've always lived in the same city. We saw each other every week. We talked every day on the phone. She was in a car accident . . . hit by a drunk in a pickup truck who pulled out in front of her . . . and just like that she was gone . . . .''

She paused, squeezing her eyes shut tightly against the tears.

''Believe me, Reverend Jones, my life was already empty before Mother died. But I haven't been able to get over her death. I can't shake the sadness. I go to bed with it. I get up with it. I don't know what to do. Will I ever get over the loss?''

Amy glanced up as she spoke the last sentence, then quickly looked down again.

''Fortunately, Mrs. Wortham, you chose something I can help you with. You will get over the death of your mother. Grief works itself out of the human spirit in time. I know it's hard for you to accept now, but as time continues to pass, your mother's death will be easier to accept, and the memories of her will become fonder and not as painful. But this doesn't mean you should simply wait out the period of grief. There are some things you should be doing now.''

Amy lifted her head, and the questioning look on her face made it unnecessary for her to speak.

''Let me tell you the first thing you can do. If I were a doctor this moment, I would prescribe one of the best cures for sorrow there is . . . and that's to cry.''

I got up from my chair, walked around and leaned against the edge of the desk, looking down at her. ''Mrs. Wortham, do you realize that since the first moment you walked in that door, you've been fighting to keep from crying? I don't know whether you do that with everyone else, but you're going to strip your emotional gears if you aren't careful. God gave you tear ducts so you could use them. Ulcers, heart attacks, and all kinds of bad things can be caused by going against the grain of your emotions.''

Her shoulders drew forward and both hands moved toward her mouth with the handkerchief clenched between them. Her hand trembled as she still strained to hold back the tears. ''But my husband and my children already think I'm weak. They look at me as if I'm almost a basket case. They've just been waiting for me to collapse after my mother's death. So I've been determined not to do it . . . .''

No longer able to hold back the flood, Amy buried her face in her hands and sobbed. Her body shook compulsively. I walked to the corner table, took a pitcher from the tray, and poured her a glass of water. Setting it on the desk in front of her and returning to my chair, I resisted the temptation to say anything too soon. She had been keeping everything bottled up inside her too long. Whether or not she would make it to Friday, I knew a good cry would at least get her through Monday.

Finally, she regained her composure and blew her nose.

"Mrs. Wortham, please don't let your first sentence be an apology. One of the best cures for sorrow is crying. Don't keep emotions like that stored up inside you. There's a time to laugh and a time to weep. My son would say there's a time to let it all hang out.

"Perhaps it would help if I tried to explain the nature of sorrow. Sorrow usually stems from two sources; either we are feeling sorry for ourselves from a selfish sense of loss or, as in the case of your mother, we believe there was more we could or should have done. I don't think the first source applies to you, so let's talk about the second. Much of our sadness seems to stem from guilt. But no amount of tears or self-punishment is going to change the past. Your remorse over the possibility that you could have done more for your mother is wasted because she is dead. It's also wasted on those around you because no one is comfortable with sadness. And it's wasted on yourself since you can't benefit by remaining sad. Your guilt is a senseless waste of time."

"But, Reverend Jones, a person just can't stop feeling there was more she could have done."

"Maybe not, but you can rechannel or recycle that energy toward the loved ones you still have around you. Let me give an exercise that will help cure your sorrow. Every time you think about what you wish you could have done, immediately ask yourself this: 'What can I do today, this very moment, for those around me I love who are still here?'

"Mrs. Wortham, most of us are guilty of either living in the past or in the future, but few of us do a good job of enjoying the sweetness of each precious moment we have each day with those we love."

Leaning forward in my chair, I continued, "I know of a woman about your age who recently was sitting on her living room floor looking at her high school annual and her college yearbook. Suddenly, she began to cry. When one of her daughters asked what was wrong, she replied, 'I let it all slip by so fast and never worked at getting the most out of each one of these experiences.'

"What I'm saying, Mrs. Wortham, is that ninety percent of our sorrow is caused by letting time get away from us without trying to get the most out of the experiences that are ours from day to day. When time takes someone from us, we can hardly keep from wondering: Could we have done more? Could we have lived more? Could we have enjoyed more?"

I paused to let these words sink in.

"You're probably thinking that now your children are gone, they don't need their mother anymore," I continued. "The truth is, your children may need you more now than they ever have. But you're going to have to work a little harder at staying in touch with them and making the moments between you count."

"Reverend Jones, I think I know what you mean, about my children, that is. I think I've been more concerned about how they feel towards me than I have about their own needs and desires. I want to be more of a help to them. But I still feel so locked in. My world seems so small that it's closing in on me."

"Then why don't you make your world a little larger? Here's an assignment which may help you cope with future sorrows in your life. Watch for those times when your friends are experiencing sorrow, then tell them that God cares. Because you see, Mrs. Wortham, He does care. He cares for them just as He cares for you. It is important for you to develop the habit of saying those words to others — God cares. If you say them often enough to people in their times of sorrow, the next time you are confronted with heartache, your own words will come back to comfort you — God cares."

"You probably feel I've been rather selfish about my own sorrow," Amy sniffed.

"In a sense, all sorrow is a form of selfishness, but that doesn't mean it is wrong or unhealthy. We simply must not indulge ourselves too long. We must remember our lives are lived in the present and that other people need us just as we need them. You will learn that you have a reserve called sympathy. The more you use it on behalf of others the less you will be tempted to use it for yourself."

"I feel better about my mother. I probably did all I could for her. I spent as much time with her as I could. Perhaps much of my sorrow has been self-indulgent, but there are still many things troubling me."

"I think we should stay at the job while we both have the matter fresh in our minds," I smiled and stood to my feet. "Why don't you get a bite of lunch and be back here at 1:30 this afternoon, and we'll talk some more?"

"I would like that if it isn't too much trouble for you," replied Amy.

"No trouble at all, Mrs. Wortham. We may have a lot of ground to cover, but Friday is still a long way off."

As she left, I thought about our play on the idea of making it to Friday. Would this be the last day I would ever see Amy Wortham?

The Legion

—————— 2 ——————

Monday, 12:00 Noon

Over lunch I thought a great deal about Mrs. Wortham and her problems, trying to get my role in her treatment into perspective. At this point, I did not see the need for psychiatric help. I had learned long ago not to play God or doctor with someone else's life.

Mrs. Wortham's plight was not unusual. Without underestimating her personal condition, which was obviously serious, I found it sobering to think that her problems were most likely shared by a large percentage of men and women her age.

Maybe this was the reason I made the decision—which Mrs. Wortham need not know was out of the ordinary to devote as much time as necessary to her case. I determined to use the whole week to get to the outer edges, at least—if not to the bottom of the invisible enemy tearing at her mind, soul, spirit and health.

Mentally I began listing the words which defined the human conditions I saw or sensed in Amy—words like guilt, fear, discouragement, worry, despair. Somehow they all seemed inadequate to express the agony she was suffering. But what other way was there to prove for the enemy lurking in the darkness of her spirit, bringing confusion and division? Little wonder when Jesus asked the demon in the man from Gadara to identify himself, he replied, "Call me Legion, for *we* are many!"

Somehow I had a compelling feeling that Mrs. Wortham had been sent to me for a reason. At least I could not help treating her that way.

Perhaps I was responding to my own sense of guilt. Too often I had become impatient with people's problems. The answer seemed simple enough to me: "Trust God and do your best!" Maybe trust was too big a step for a damaged soul.

A wise surgeon never likes to operate until the surrounding infection can be controlled. First, Amy's fever would have to be brought down. Then perhaps she would be ready to accept faith. To accomplish this, I would have to lead her through the haunted house of life in the light of day. She had to see that the ghosts terrorizing her life were inside her and not in the house.

Discussing her sorrow over her mother's death had been a surface exercise. I determined to get to the root of her problem, a challenge which left me with a sense of inadequacy.

How to Overcome Guilt

— 3 —

Monday, 1:30 P.M.

She was back promptly at 1:30, looking even more dejected than when she had left. Her words did not surprise me.

"Reverend Jones, I appreciated our talk this morning, but I'm keeping you from more important things. Perhaps we should leave matters as they are for awhile. Maybe, as you said, time will take care of my problems."

Sensing I was about to lose her I cut deep.

"Mrs. Wortham, why don't you say what's really on your mind? You don't believe we got anywhere this morning. You think we wasted time talking about an obvious situation which gave you no relief. You wanted quick, easy answers that would clear up everything at once.

"You are like the person who spends a year gaining forty-five pounds and wants to know how to lose it in one day.

"You are right about one thing—I don't have any time to waste, and neither do you. But there are no easy answers, and time alone isn't going to solve your problems.

"You can decide to walk out of here, and we will never see each other again. Or we can tackle your life and see what comes of it. I want to try. I'm not a medicine man nor a miracle worker, but I do believe in both—medicine and miracles. I will tell you everything I know, believe, and think.

"If you're willing to devote the time to the task, I'm ready. But don't try to put the responsibility for what you decide to do on me. It's *your* decision and *your* life."

She smiled for the first time, which made her appear years younger.

"Now you're beginning to sound like my oldest daughter," she grinned. "I'm ready if you are. But we must settle on a fee for your time. That'll make me feel better about our sessions."

"Mrs. Wortham, I have two fees: expensive and free. Neither of the two involves money. If we get nowhere, the experience will have been expensive for both of us. If we make it to Friday, perhaps there will be value for both of us. Frankly, I need these sessions as much as you. We ministers tend to answer questions no one is asking. So you and I may be able to help each other. Let's just see where all this takes us, which leads me to ask if you have any questions from our meeting this morning?"

Amy started to look down and then, as if abruptly changing her mind, she faced me with her words.

"I don't know how to put it in a simple question. I feel terribly guilty. I don't mean about my mother. I know I did all I could. I miss her, that's all.

"But I carry a lot of guilt about other matters— my children, my marriage, my 'habits.' Do I need to get more specific?"

I nodded.

"Okay," she continued with a sigh. "I have not always been true to my husband. I have been using liquor as an escape—or whatever. Lots of things I've done make me feel ashamed. I somehow reconcile all my problems as some sort of punishment. What do I do about my guilt over real sins? What do I do about my past and present mistakes?''

I waited until she had stopped thinking about all she had just said and was ready to listen. Then I spoke, slowly, and deliberately.

''You forget them. It's just that simple. I didn't say easy, but simple. Before you fault me for being over simplistic, let me say this: *You can't change history!* Nothing you do, say, or feel is going to alter what has been done. Indulging yourself in feelings of remorse is a waste of time. Your shame, guilt, and remorse will change nothing. The only way to deal with your past is to learn to forget.''

I paused to give her a chance to respond, knowing it was important not to get ahead of her.

''You mean . . . I should simply begin *acting* as if things that happened in the past didn't happen?''

''That's exactly what I do *not* mean. That's not forgetting, but *repression*,'' I returned, leaning forward in my chair. ''Nothing is ever gained by acting like things never happened. We can't ignore the past. That's like putting a barking dog in the basement. You always know he's there. You never know when he will come bursting out to embarrass you. The past sometimes has a way of doing that.

''Furthermore, repression breeds other ills. When you push an experience into your subconscious mind, it will usually reappear in a different form. For instance, a short temper often is nothing more than a repressed act of the past resurfacing in the guise of anger. When I use the term *forget*, I mean repentance.''

"Reverend Jones, I'm familiar with what preachers call repentance, and I . . . .''

"Forgive my interrupting, Mrs. Wortham, but I don't think you *do* understand repentance or you would not be living with your guilt.

"Repentance is more than merely being sorry you did something wrong. It is coming clean before God and confessing the matter that concerns you. Call it by name. Admit your mistake. And then . . . *listen to this* . . . walk away from it! Leave it at His feet. And in return, accept the most marvelous luxury God offers—forgiveness!''

"Reverend Jones, I don't understand forgiveness! And I don't trust it!'' She responded bitterly, "I just don't believe in it—at least not for me.''

"Let me offer a reason why you find forgiveness—God's forgiveness—difficult to accept,'' I offered. "It's because you see so little of it around you. People are poor forgivers. We find it hard to forgive each other. When we do offer forgiveness to others, we tend not to forget. And by not forgetting, we cancel out the offer of forgiveness.

"But that isn't how God operates. When you truly lay a deed before Him and repent of it, He not only forgives you, but promises to look upon you as though the deed had never happened!''

"But how can people ever be sure they have received forgiveness?''

Hope began to dawn in her eyes. Now we were getting somewhere! I forced myself to slow down and wait for a second before answering.

"There are two ways to go about it, Mrs. Wortham. First, you learn to look upon yourself differently. You say, 'If God has forgiven me, I am going to forgive myself.' Second, you begin forgiving others. You see, God's forgiveness is like electricity, it cannot get into you unless it can get out of you."

I paused. Was I going too fast? Was I making everything sound too simple and easy?

"Reverend Jones, I think I follow what you're saying. But I must be honest. What good is God's forgiveness if others don't forgive you?"

"Okay, let's settle something now. We are not going to concern ourselves with matters which are beyond our control. How other people think, feel, and react is absolutely beyond our control. Do you understand this? Do you realize you can drive yourself crazy trying to change other people?

"Believe me, we're going to have our hands full changing the way *you* think, much less others. So let's just concentrate on these four questions. Number one: Do you want God's forgiveness? Number two: Do you believe God will do what He promises? Number three: Will you accept God's forgiveness? Number four: Are you willing to forgive others, even if they don't forgive you?

"These four things are all that matter because you alone control the answer to all of them. I'm not interested in discussing how to change our sick, unforgiving, self-righteous, and judgmental society. I'm only interested in *you* and what you think—about yourself, your past, your future . . . and God."

Amy didn't answer. Realizing I had gone too far,

too fast, I got out of my chair, walked around the desk and sat in the chair beside her.

"Look, Mrs. Wortham, I'm not trying to get you on your knees. I'm not trying to wrap things up in a quick, neat bundle. We have much ground to cover and we haven't even scratched the surface. But if we can't drive down a few pegs as we move along, we are just going to drift. We still have the present and the future to deal with, and maybe even some more of the past. But there is no need for you to spend one more day with a defeated, guilt-ridden attitude."

I was pressing again. When would I ever learn?

"What do you want me to do, Reverend Jones?"

I could kick myself. The preacher in me was about to blow everything . . . always pushing for a victory.

"You're doing fine. Pardon me if it appeared that I was pressing. I know it sounds simplistic to ask you to forget the past, but sooner or later that's what you have to do. It may not be today, or tomorrow—but you will have to do it. People who fail to forget, or forget to forget, or refuse to forget are keeping frustration alive and inviting despair. There is only one place where the past belongs, and that's in the past."

I stood. "Let's take a break, and meet again at four o'clock."

"Today?" she winced. "I mean, are you sure you have time for more of my problems today?"

"Mrs. Wortham, Monday is almost gone, and we have miles to go before Friday."

"I'll be back," she sighed, starting for the door. Pausing, she smiled nervously, "Will you tell me

the moment you think I'm a hopeless case? I mean
. . . I feel there is something you wanted of me . . .
some response . . . and I don't feel anything. I'm
kind of bewildered about our time together. I'm
pleased, of course. But I don't want to disappoint
you . . . and nothing has changed.'' Her eyes
dropped. ''I know that isn't what you want to
hear.''

''Mrs. Wortham, all I ask is that you hang onto
your honesty. For now, you may think it's not
much of an asset but in the end, it could be our
best ally. All I want for now is to see you again at
four o'clock.''

I returned to my desk, but couldn't think of
starting anything else. I had seen Amy twice and
had made no apparent headway. One more strike,
and I would be out—at least for Monday. *Why do I
always start preaching? Answers, answers, answers. Why do I have to have so many answers?*

Perhaps I was being too hard on myself . . . at
least she was coming back.

Working Through Loneliness

4

Monday, 4:00 P.M.

Four o'clock came, but no Mrs. Wortham.

I had been anticipating her arrival since 3:45, so each minute past the time she was expected seemed even longer. At 4:15, I left the office and walked past the receptionist's desk, hoping to find her. Failing to see her I strode back through the building to the parking lot in the rear.

Amy was sitting in her car. She saw me but made no effort to get out. Without comment, I opened the door and got in beside her. Finally she broke the silence, both hands on the wheel, looking ahead as though she were driving.

"Reverend Jones, I am a very, *very* lonely woman. You might say I am a lonely old woman, but it isn't the age which distinguishes me—only the loneliness. My children are gone, my mother is gone, and my husband is rarely at home. But that isn't it.

"I'm lonely when I play bridge with other women. That feeling never leaves. When I go to a party, it's there. When I shop in a crowded store, loneliness goes with me. Wherever I go, there is this void which swallows me up. It almost speaks to me . . . reaches out to me. I can almost see it. I can't touch it but, oh God, can I feel it!

"When I'm alone, as I have been this past hour, I am so keenly aware of it. I even say out loud, 'I am lonely.' "

I started to address her as "Mrs. Wortham," but caught myself, thinking how impersonal it sounded.

"At the risk of sounding trite, you must know you are not alone in your sense of loneliness," I began slowly and quietly.

"Loneliness afflicts both men and women, those of status as well as the derelicts, the adolescents and the aged, the single and the married, the learned and the illiterate—and I might add, even the clergy—not to mention those forgotten by society in prisons or hospitals or on skid row. No, you are not alone in your loneliness."

I was fishing. I did not want to lecture, just to listen—to talk *with* her, not *to* her. But failing to get a foothold, I forged ahead, hoping to find some conversational pivot that might cause her to say, "I hadn't thought of it that way."

"The frightening part is that our society is set up to exploit the lonely—to create situations to attract the lonely. We have dance studios, health salons, and private parties for the purpose of meeting people. Our society is filled with those who traffic in boredom—those who profit from promising that time will be consumed for those who pay the price.

"On every corner there's a bar, where night after night the same people sit side by side on rows of stools—monuments to loneliness."

Amy continued to stare straight ahead as I continued. "Even prostitution and homosexuality become escapes from loneliness for all involved— both the one buying and the one selling. All these endeavors become dead ends, though, because they fill time, but not the void."

She relaxed her hands from the grip of the wheel. Leaning her head back against the seat, eyes closed, she looked like a little girl.

"How does one fill the void?" Amy's voice came barely above a whisper. It seemed she wanted to say more, but didn't because the effort would be too great. She appeared tired rather than engulfed with emotion. In fact, the lack of emotion was almost chilling.

Maybe I was reading too much into the setting. It occurred to me that this could be her way to solve loneliness—to spend time seeking out a listening ear. Perhaps I was taking everything too serious, looking for the dramatic! After all, I knew little about her . . . nothing except what she had told me.

"Perhaps another drink would help," I baited. She had hinted in our phone conversation that she had been drinking. So I brought it up—still fishing for an approach to take with our discussion.

"Don't think I didn't consider it," she mumbled, eyes still closed. "But if I had gone home, I would never have returned."

"Maybe a drink would help you to forget that your loneliness is not the absence of others, but your presence among others where it is treated as absence," I said bluntly.

"Perhaps another drink will help you forget that you are regarded as dead. Perhaps another drink will let you forget you are forgotten."

I was looking for a fight—an argument—anything which would put life in her.

"I'm not an alcoholic, Reverend Jones, at least not yet. But I could be very easily. In fact, I might welcome it.''

Her words faded into a wry, humorless laugh. ''Forgotten, eh? Regarded as dead? I should be so lucky! The truth is, I don't consider myself *regarded* at all. Only the void is real. So what else can you suggest besides a drink, *Reverend Jones?*''

She used my name with the same careful intent that I had avoided hers. There was at least a little fight left in her.

''You might consider sex. At least you will not be alone, though you probably will still be lonely,'' I shot back.

She smiled, her eyes still closed. Amy was still a beautiful woman, and she knew it.

''Is that a proposition, preacher?''

I let the question pass. She knew it wasn't offered seriously and needed no response.

''You've tried marriage. Is this a part of your problem or your solution? You have told me nothing of your husband.''

''My marriage is not worth the paper it's written on. What is there to tell? He's a successful man; self-made, self-motivated, self-centered; spends half his time away working and the other half just away. What happens to me is neither because of him nor despite him. I don't love him—I don't hate him. How we drifted apart is not the incredible thing, but how we ever got together. How can two teenagers make promises to each other with any assurance that they can or will want to keep them twenty-five years later?''

This wasn't the time or place for marital counseling. No use trying to make two into one if you cannot make one into one.

"You can always seek out counseling. Maybe if we search your past long enough, we can find someone you can blame yourself on."

She opened her eyes and glared at me. "I'm beginning to think I made a poor choice, Reverend Jones. So far you've only made snide suggestions, which we both know have nothing to do with what we're talking about. Surely you can do more than prey on what little you know about me!"

A spark.

"And then, of course, you can always pity yourself. Why not? Everybody else does."

She settled back, her hands on the wheel.

"I suppose self-pity does figure in. But what else is there . . . when no one else . . . ."

She turned, facing me.

"Reverend Jones, do you have a first name? Larry. Larry Jones. Right? Larry, can you give me ten practical things a person might do to overcome loneliness? Let's just suppose you were assigning homework for a child," she snapped.

"Certainly I could if I thought it would do any good."

She reached in her purse and took a dollar bill in her hand. "I'll give you a dime for each one."

I had misgivings about the exercise, but I felt she was buying time—time that I needed as much as she.

"First, make plans to see three people you have known and liked but have lost contact with," I began. "Second, make a list of your interests in an effort to uncover a hobby. Third, make a list of people you know who are lonely and ask each of them to do something with you. Fourth, write letters to three old friends you have neglected. Fifth, do one good turn for someone each day. Sixth, be on the lookout for new places to go. Seventh, always have something to look forward to. Eighth, don't expect too much too soon. Ninth, deal with your loneliness a bit at a time. Find ways to get through an hour . . . and then a day.''

''And ten?''

''Nine is all I know, and I don't have change so you can keep your dollar.''

She was leaning back again, eyes closed.

''Larry Jones, you can't offer things like those to a basket case. Surely there's more in that head of yours than trying to turn a middle-aged misfit into a pen pal.''

''There's more, Amy, if you are willing to accept your solitude and build on it.''

''Such as?''

''Such as this for starters: You are alone and yet you are never alone.''

She was looking at me again, and it was I who leaned back with eyes closed.

''Let me tell you about a friend of mine,'' I continued. The rumor was that He was born out of wedlock . . . which wasn't true, but He had to grow up with it nonetheless. He was completely misunderstood by His parents. He became a minister but was later disowned by His church. In time, His friends left Him. One of His best friends betrayed Him.

''He was later falsely accused on criminal charges, tried and sentenced to death. During His execution, He even thought He was forsaken by

God. He died with His mother weeping at His side.''

"He spent most of His adult life alone, forsaken by friends, family and peers. And all He ever accomplished was to alter the history of the human race. For He built His life on a promise . . . that He would never leave Amy Wortham alone. Never. Never forsake her. Always stay beside her . . . guide her . . . comfort her.''

She laid her head in her hands on the steering wheel.

"Oh, Larry . . .'' she began to cry. "If only . . . .'' The tears came faster.

"Amy, Jesus loves you. He cares for you. I know this doesn't fill up all the empty space this very moment. But He can fill the void in your life if you will only let Him.''

She stopped crying and reached in her purse for her handkerchief.

"I must go. I really must.''

"But, Amy . . . .''

"Please.''

I opened the door. "It's been a long day. Amy, I feel I have known you a long time. And do you realize it's still only Monday?'' Will you come back in the morning? Nine o'clock?''

"Yes, I'll be here. But I must go now.''

I got out of the car, shut the door and started walking away.

"Larry.''

"Yes?'' Turning towards her.

"Thanks.''

Worry Is a Waste of Time

5

Tuesday, 9:00 A.M.

The buzzer rang on the intercom.

"There's an Amy Wortham on the line for you."

"Hello," cheerfully, punching the line with the blinking light.

"Is this Larry Jones?"

"Yes."

"I mean is this the Reverend Larry Jones?"

"Speaking."

"Well, Larry Jones, I called to tell you I'm giving you the day off."

"Amy, I'm waiting for you. We don't have time for a day off."

"Well, Larry Jones, I don't think we better plan . . ." the phone made sounds like it was being juggled from one hand to the other ". . . on today. You see, Larry Jones, I haven't dressed."

"I'll wait. We'll make it 10 o'clock . . . or 11."

"Well, Larry, you see . . . I've got this problem. I'm not well . . . I'm . . . I mean . . . well, Larry, I'm drunk! Can you believe that? I've been awake since early . . . I went to sleep drunk . . . and I woke up sober . . . and now I'm drunk again."

"I'll wait, Amy, I'm not going to lose this day. You asked me to help you make it to Friday, and

I'm not going to let you cheat me out of a day. So take a cold shower, drink some coffee and get down here."

Silence. But I could hear some kind of movement.

"Amy?"

"Larry, I'm going to spend today practicing . . . pract . . . tic . . . cing solitude. I want to be alone! Get it? I mean . . . I can't do it . . . I just can't get up and do it."

"Amy, where do you live? I'm coming out there." Silence. "Amy, I'll look you up in the phone book, so tell me."

"Larry, you don't want to come out here. I don't, oh . . . I don't want to do it today . . . I just don't want to."

"Okay, I'll find it myself. Get a shower. I'm coming . . . now!"

After finding the address; I stopped by the house and picked up my wife. When we arrived at Amy's, I told Frances to wait for me in the car. This was my first house call in years except in crusades.

I rang the doorbell, but there was no answer. I opened the door and walked into the den. Amy was sitting on the sofa with her feet propped on the coffee table, a drink in her hand. She had dressed, but that was as far as she had gotten.

"Have a s . . . seat, preacher. It's almost time for the meetin' to start. I'm the first . . . drunk on the program. Fix yourself a drink. Oh gosh, I'm fresh out of grape juice," she giggled. "Isn't that what you guys drink?"

I went into the kitchen to see if coffee had been fixed. No luck. I opened the refrigerator and got a

Tab, returned to the den, and took a seat opposite her.

"Well, preacher, now you know how the other half lives. Not a bad layout for a little old girl from Lawton, Oklahoma, huh? Oh God, I'm tired. Couldn't you come back after . . . something."

"Amy, we had a deal. I want you to know I'm a busy person . . . ."

"Big deal!" she mocked.

" . . . and I cleared this whole week for you. I didn't call you . . . you called me. And you aren't going to get rid of me as easily as you think."

She started to get up, then fell back onto the sofa, spilling her drink.

"You'd think I wouldn't waste good whiskey," she giggled again. "Larry, why don't preachers drink? I mean, you gotta have a *little* fun now and then."

"Amy, is this fun?"

"No, it isn't fun yet," her face twisted into a scowl, "because I can still hear you and see you . . . and still think and feel. But a few more of these, and the thinking goes . . . and the feeling—and you, too."

She looked at her almost empty glass and carefully reached over to the bottle of vodka and poured herself another drink—straight.

"Amy, that's why I'm here . . . ."

"Why are you here, Reverend Jones? To talk? Talk, talk, talk. Well, I had enough talk yesterday to last me 'til Friday. Now I just . . . want . . . to be left . . . alone. . . ."

"Amy, if. . . ."

"And don't tell me any more about loneliness

because you don't know anything about it. Junk . . .
everything you said was junk . . . write a friend . . .
Jesus loves me . . . this I know . . . 'cause the Bible
tells me so . . . junk! So why don't you leave me to
my precious loneliness? What's in it for you? What
do you want? Am I a game you preachers play? Do
you get your pay docked when you lose a cus-
tomer?"

"Amy!" I almost surprised myself at the loud-
ness of my voice.

"I'm number ten, don't you see?" I got up and
walked to the fireplace, turned and stooped before
the coffee table looking her in the eye.

"You asked for ten ways to overcome loneliness
and I gave you nine because you didn't need
words. You needed a person who cares, someone
reaching out to you in love to whom you could also
reach. I could have given you my sermon on loneliness, but you didn't need it. You needed me . . .
someone like me who cares . . . and I care."

I sat beside her on the sofa.

"Amy, we're all a mob of hermits. There is the
hermit within us because we are selfish by nature.
And there is a mob within us which causes us to
seek comradery. But the whole system fouls up
unless we can teach solitude to the hermit and relationship to the mob.

"Right now your insides are damaged. You
don't have the strength or will to find value in
being alone, and you don't have the faith to trust
God's presence. So the one thing I can offer your
loneliness is me—a real live person who cares
about Amy Wortham—and you don't even trust
that. If you can't crawl out of your loneliness for

one day, then please let me crawl in with you because I love you . . . as God loves you . . . and as others would love you if you would just let go and receive love.''

''Reverend Jones, you say you love me; why you don't even know me.'' She was speaking more clearly but her hand was shaking so badly she could hardly hold her glass.

''I want to know you better, Amy.''

''Really? Then how's this for knowing me better? My dear husband . . . the father of my children, wants a divorce. My strong protector and provider wants out! And do you know what we have to divide between us? Debts! We owe money on everything — house, cars, doctors, even our food and clothes!

''And who am I? A woman who hasn't worked a day in her adult life . . . never drawn a paycheck with my name on it. I'm a woman with a house that I won't be able to live in, a car that I won't be able to drive. How will I survive? Be a cocktail waitress? Can't stay sober. Be a secretary? Can't type.''

She got up and stumbled out of the room, returning shortly with a bundle of papers which she dropped on the coffee table before sitting back down.

''These, Larry, are bills.'' She rubbed her forehead with her glass. ''Some of them are six months old. My husband doesn't even know how much we owe. He just pays the ones who threaten him the loudest. Besides, he barely has enough to take care of his girlfriend.

''What I'm saying is that if we stay together, we

won't make it and if we get a divorce, *I* won't make it. Six months, either way. We won't make it, together or apart, another six months. That is, unless you know something I don't,'' she smirked, leaning back on the sofa, and staring at the wall across from her.

I walked into the kitchen and began looking for the makings of coffee. A ''Mr. Coffee'' made the job easier. I didn't want the coffee as much as I did a break. I was getting nowhere . . . fast, I was losing ground, the battle, the war, the whole thing. It wasn't that Amy kept new problems coming, rather that I couldn't get the thing turned around.

I carried two cups of coffee back to the den, set them on the coffee table, and again took the seat almost directly across the table from Amy. Her eyes were still focused on the painting above the fireplace.

''Yes, Amy, I do know something you don't. At the risk of sounding like a preacher, I'm not going to let you back me down from what I believe with all my heart.''

I leaned forward, hoping to get her to look at me.

''Please listen to me, Amy. One day Jesus was talking to some people just like you who were worried about how they were going to make it. He said, 'Look at the birds. They don't know from one day to the next where their food will be, but God sees that they find it.' Then He said, 'Your Heavenly Father cares even more for you.'

''Then He said, 'Look at the lilies.' The lilies remind me of you, Amy. They are even more help-less than the birds. They are tied to the ground. But He said, 'Your Heavenly Father clothes the lilies more beautifully than anything.'

"Amy, it was just an earthy way of saying that God cares more for you and me than birds and flowers, and that He is going to take care of our needs.

"And then He said something, Amy, which was meant just for you. He said, 'Look at today.'

"Amy, you talk about not making it another six months? Well, do you know what today is? Today is the day six months ago you said you would never make it to. But you made it, didn't you?

"Don't you see that worry over the future is just as needless and wasteful as guilt is about the past?"

Amy had not moved or even turned her eyes. It was like talking to a statue, but I continued anyway.

"And all He asks of you is this: 'Seek ye first the kingdom of God and His righteousness, and all these things will be added to you.' "

She looked at me.

"Larry, you have one solution for everything, don't you? Is life really so simple that you can trust God and everything turns out right?"

"No, Amy, not one solution, but the first step. For now, you are like a boat without an anchor. God can be your anchor—your vantage point— your strength to face your problems."

"Will trusting God give me back my mother, my husband, my health, my wasted years?"

"Amy, the Bible says, 'All things work together for good to them that love the Lord!' What it does not say is that everything *happens* good. There is no question that many bad things have happened to you . . . terrible things. But it does say that with your faith and God's help, things will work out for good! And they will for you, Amy, if you will just trade your big bag of worry for a small bag of faith."

She sat up, then leaned directly forward and looked at me intently.

"Larry, I'm going to be as honest with you as I think you are with me. I didn't come to you for religion — but for help. You're trying to make me cross a chasm in two jumps. The chasm is my messed-up life. One jump is your offer of trust in God, and the other is my frantic leap for survival and sanity.

"I would like to take both jumps just to please you. But I'm simply not into faith and God and those things. Most of the religious people I have known have been fakes. I've seen too much hate in God's name, too much greed in God's name, and too many lies in God's name.

"The first man who ever put the make on this young girl was our local minister. One of the deacons in our church drove my father out of business and into the grave.

"Present company excepted, I can't name three 'Christians' that I would trust with a secret, much less my life. I know none of this rules out the validity of God — at least I'm not sure — but I'm just more interested in how I, Amy Wortham, can make it, if she can.

"Let me ask you, Larry. What would you say about my 'worry,' as you call it, if you were not speaking as a minister?"

"I would say it's a stupid waste of time. Your worry isn't going to change a thing. If something bad is going to happen, your worry won't stop it.

"That's why I picked up on Friday. I want you to have a full, happy life for years to come. But I thought the farther you looked into the future, the more you compounded your anxiety. I want two things for you, Amy: to get you back to the present . . . today . . . this week . . . where your life is actually being lived; and to get new, fresh strength and courage into your life. And this is what Jesus Christ can do for you.

"It's tough to work merely at getting bad, harmful things out of your life. It's easier to put new and better ones into it which, in time, replace the things that have been pulling you down."

I looked at my watch for the first time. It was almost 1:00 in the afternoon.

"I didn't realize we had been at it this long. We both need a break." I stood to leave. We can start again about three o'clock. I don't mean to be pushy, but you owe me a visit."

Amy had been silent a long time. She had retreated on me again. I was pushing for another appointment because I had a bad feeling about things as they stood. I thought how simple it was to stand and preach where people couldn't ask questions and talk back. That way you never had to know how far you were missing the mark.

"Amy? Can you make it later?"

"I have an appointment with the doctor at three."

"Oh?"

"Six months ago I had a lump removed from my breast. Now there is another . . . same breast."

I wanted to cry. I wanted to stand up and say,

"Look, you have no right to lay this much on me. Haven't you handed me enough for one minister to deal with? Don't you know there is a three-problem limit to the people I counsel?"

"Amy, I'm sorry."

What a stupid thing to say.

"I'm afraid. I know, I know. Don't start another sermon. I just made a simple statement of fact. I am scared out of my mind. Somebody once said there are only two kinds of people, the terminally ill and the miserable. Those are my choices. I don't know which I fear most, death or deformity. Oh God, Larry, I hate being morbid. Yes, I'll come by your office straight from the doctor."

"Would you like my wife Frances to go with you? She's been out in the car for more than three hours. I'm sure she would rather be on the inside."

"Oh that poor woman! Why didn't you tell me? No. I'm glad you didn't tell me. I would love to have her go with me."

I moved toward the front door. "She will pick you up here at 2:30. Will that . . . ?"

"Give me time to take a shower? Oh, I've already sobered up, or didn't you notice?"

"Amy, pardon my saying it, but you really aren't a very successful drunk."

"Forgive my saying it, but you are a very kind and dear man."

On that note I left. Feeling good? Feeling bad? Just glad to have any feeling left. *Thank the Lord it's only Tuesday.*

Facing Fear

——— 6 ———

Tuesday, 5:00 P.M.

When I returned to my office from Amy's house, there was a plain folder on my desk marked, "*Mr. and Mrs. Paul Wortham.*" It contained the results of an investigation my secretary had made during my visit to Amy that morning. I had asked her to find out everything about the couple she could learn in a few hours. She had started with a friend who had attended school with both of them and gone from there. I was impressed with her thoroughness in the short time.

I quickly scanned the contents, then began reading the report a second time, underlining key information. Without doubt, the file gave me a fresh perspective on Amy Wortham.

Paul Wortham: graduated from Lawton High School, 1949; Oklahoma University, 1953; attended Harvard Divinity School in Cambridge, considered to be one of their brightest theological students, earning his Ph.D. in philosophy and religion in 1960. From there, he pastored two Baptist churches, five years each, one in Oklahoma and the other in Florida, before becoming a professor at a state university in the south. He later became president of a motivation company, and after that opened his own business.

Married Amy Pascal in 1953. *Amy had been a minister's wife!* Two daughters and a son. *Amy never mentioned a son.* Paul Junior was a professional golfer. Both daughters were married and living out of state.

Amy Pascal Wortham: Graduated from Lawton High School in 1948; Oklahoma University in 1952, Homecoming Queen, and Most Representative Girl her senior year. Graduated from college Magna Cum Laude; two masters' degrees: one in linguistics from University of Florida and one in counseling (counseling!) from Oklahoma University.

Daughters, Connie and Carolee, married and living out of state.

Amy Wortham, beautiful, brilliant, counselor, minister's wife. No mention of her son. Here I thought I was dealing with one person and discovered I'm dealing with another. I had formed a series of ideas about Amy, building from her weaknesses and problems back to an empty, unknown center.

Why had she not told me more about herself? Did it matter? Why had I sought more information? Obviously, it didn't matter to Amy. The Amy I knew needed saving—the one on paper didn't. Where did the Amy I know begin? What went wrong? How did she lose her faith to such an extent that she didn't even allude to it in our sessions? Did she ever have faith? Has she ever really lost it? If so, is it too late to find it again?

I put aside the report and tried for an hour to act

as though Amy Wortham didn't exist. But she did, and I could not will her away. She was ever present in my thoughts.

"Mrs. Wortham is here to see you."

"Have her come in."

How she could do to herself what she had done, men will never understand about women. Surely she had been motivated by Frances. Amy was ravishing. She was dressed in a full white skirt and bright blue blouse, with a sailor bow low across her shoulders. Her hair was beneath a scarf, her eyes framed with a brightness which made her sparkle. Amy's lips were matched by the flush in her cheeks. I felt strangely proud of her and didn't know why.

She sat across from the desk and smiled. I still didn't know what to expect from her. Was it that I no longer saw the meek, downtrodden housewife, but the beauty, counselor, scholar that her records had revealed?

Only when she began to speak did I remember the Amy I was dealing with.

"Do you remember the story of the man who saw a sign which read, 'Cheer up, things could be worse,' so he cheered up and sure enough, things got worse?" she began.

"Meaning?"

"The lump has to be removed. The sooner the better. The odds are strong that the breast will have to go this time."

"But you don't *know* that."

"I know the odds are strong . . . ."

"But did the doctor actually say, 'The breast will have to be removed.'?"

Amy stood and stepped to the window, making a pretense at looking out. She turned again and paced from object to object in the room, first looking at a picture, then studying the pages of a book.

"No, Larry, he didn't use those exact words—but he implied them."

"How, Amy? Tell me what he said."

"It was his manner. I could tell he was disturbed about having to go back in so soon."

"How was he disturbed, Amy? Did he bite his nails? What did he do or say to make you think he was disturbed?"

She swung around, glaring at me, then casually sat, picked up a magazine, and began to leaf through it.

"I could tell."

I leaned forward, resting my elbows on the desk, to keep my voice as free of strain as possible.

"How could you tell? Did you ask him if he thought your breast would have to be removed?"

"Yes, I asked him!" she snapped.

"And what did he say?"

"Oh, what do doctors always say . . . 'let's don't cross bridges, etc.' "

"But didn't he explain that it isn't unusual for a woman to have a second lump removed from her breast without it being any more serious than the first? I know a number of women who've had a second lump removed. I can't believe he gave you any cause for unnecessary alarm. I would even be willing to guess the odds favor nothing more severe than your initial operation."

"Larry, do you realize how insignificant odds are

to a woman in this predicament? What if they are a thousand to one in my favor? It only takes one! And even the thought . . . the possibility . . . terrifies me! Can't you see that? When I picture myself having . . . not having—I can't stand it! I *won't* stand it. I don't know what . . . I feel like I'm going to throw up.''

"Amy, I understand your fear, and I see the facts as they are as well as the possibilities. But we have to keep them all separate. Let's put aside the possibilities for a moment. The facts are: one, you have had one lump removed without serious repercussions; two, you are going to have a second lump removed; three, you have no evidence to support any difficulty beyond this point.

"Those are the facts—no more—no less. So you are afraid, not of the facts as you know them, but rather of uncertain, but serious possibilities. If you are not careful, your fear will hurt you more than all the facts and possibilities combined.''

"Then, I should not be afraid." She shook her head. "So easy for a man to say."

"Amy, let me tell you about a man named Howard Grisholm. He lived in an apartment in the lower East Side of New York. Awakening one night with a stabbing pain in his stomach, he went into his bathroom in the dark and took what he thought was medicine. It didn't taste right. He turned on the light and was dismayed that he had drunk rat poison.

"He raced to the phone and called the hospital, which was only five blocks away. The ambulance came. But when they arrived at the hospital, Grisholm was dead.

"The doctor discovered that the rat poison wasn't that strong. An autopsy was performed. Grisholm had suffered a cardiac arrest. The doctor's diagnosis was that the man had died of fear."

"I get your point, preacher, only I don't think my fear is quite the killing kind at this stage."

"No, but it is the crippling kind. It is a negative factor that is contributing to your emotional paralysis."

She was back into her looking-toward-the-ceiling posture.

"Larry, why don't you come out and say it. I simply have too many problems for any normal person," she spat.

I leaned back, never taking my eyes from her, sensing that lack of eye contact slowed down our progress.

"I wouldn't agree with the phrase 'too many' and I don't see you as being abnormal. You are like a person who, being in a weakened physical condition, becomes susceptible to all kinds of germs and you're emotionally vulnerable. I think the cure for one problem, if it can be found and accepted, could lead to a healthier outlook in several areas. So let's not scatter our shot with generalizations about the vastness of your dilemma. Let's stay with the subject of your fear for awhile and see where it leads. I'm interested in what you fear and why."

She gazed at me. When would I be able to get a handle on the significance of when she looked and when she didn't?

"There is nothing to fear but fear itself, eh?"

she mocked, smiling.

"Wrong. There are all kinds of things to fear, and there are an endless number of things people do fear. I think the dictionary lists more than seventy-five different phobias. They are all real to the persons experiencing them."

"Seventy-five?"

"More. There's *acrophobia*, the fear of high places; *agoraphobia*, the fear of open places; *claustrophobia*, the fear of closed places; *ergophobia*, the fear of work; *neophobia*, the fear of new things; *pathophobia*, the fear of disease; and on and on. Finally, there's *phobophobia*, which is the fear of everything."

"You're losing me. I don't see the point of all this."

"The point is, people can go through life being afraid and never really know what it is they fear. Or worse still, they know they're afraid, but they don't know what to do about it."

"I know what I fear, and there isn't anything I can do about it. It's that simple," Amy mumbled.

"Is it? Then tell me what you fear."

"Does saying it make it better? I fear losing a breast on the one hand and cancer on the other. So, what's new?"

"I think it's deeper than that. You fear these two things all right, but it goes deeper than that. Wouldn't you agree, regarding the loss of a breast, that it is failure you truly fear?"

"I'm afraid, if I can use the word, you are going to have to explain yourself."

Her eyes were riveted on me at the one time I sincerely wished that she were looking away.

"Okay, I'll try. And if I get out of line, or offend you in any way, please stop me. As I see it, your breasts are important to you for two reasons: because they enhance your appearance and because of the role they play in sex.

"Let's take the matter of cosmetics first. Women these days are having all kinds of surgical adjustments to improve their figures, both with their clothes on and off . . . ." I was blushing.

"Amy, this is very difficult for me, and if you'd rather . . . ."

Without smiling she said, "Larry, would you please continue and stop worrying about me!"

I could cut out my tongue. Here I was trying to play down the significance of her problem and my attitude was confirming her concern.

"Well, some women want larger breasts," I began again. "Some want smaller ones. Others who were absolutely flat chested are being given normal looking bustlines. And I am not talking merely about 'problem surgery.' Some models and actresses have face lifts, eye jobs, and breast surgery because they already look good and want to look better.

"So much for looks. It also is possible, through surgery, for a cosmetically constructed breast to feel normal to a man's touch. The major loss is the feeling for the woman and the sense of loss in her mind."

"Larry, this all sounds good in theory, but a woman cannot be easily convinced that a man will not be turned off . . . if not repelled . . . by a substitute for the real thing. Anyway, silicone for a superstar is a lot different from one being real and one being false.''

I continued, ''Enter the fear of failure. You're scared about an abrupt setback in your sex appeal. You've already had this damaged by the problems with your husband. Now, you face the possibility of a new experience with another man or the task of reclaiming romance with your husband. Either way, you are confronted with tackling personal relationships knowing that you aren't what you used to be.''

''To put it bluntly, that's about it. Rather bleak, wouldn't you say?'' replied Amy.

''In a way, Amy, your situation is similar— though much more extreme—to what a man experiences when his hair begins to fall out, his stomach protrudes, the bifocals come, the teeth go, and he watches his sexual prowess slowly slipping away.

''I want to say one more thing on this subject: I have grown weary of the constant emphasis on sex and of the intense interest in how people look these days.

''Somehow we must search for beauty inside the human spirit, which brings me to say: I think you are a truly beautiful person. You are honest and sensitive. You have charm and grace and intelligence.

''You are a person worth loving and having someone to love. And if you will only see yourself through these dark days, learn to love and accept yourself as you are, you will see better days. I promise you that. Because you are indeed, Amy Wortham, a cut above the human race around you. And this holds true with or without your present physical structure, which is also well above average, I might add.''

Amy was still looking at me. It seemed she was determined not to look away. Her eyes were glistening with tears though she was smiling.

''Larry, no man has spoken words like that to me in years . . . if ever. I don't know if it's the preacher in you or what else motivated it, but words like that go a long way with a woman. You are a good man for saying them. I only wish I had the courage to believe them.''

''The other fear, Amy, is the big one. Your fear of death: It's there, and in time we must talk about it, for it is behind everything—cancer, loneliness, worry, guilt, love, sorrow. Death lurkes behind each of these, and the fear of it is tormenting.''

''Or the fascination with it,'' she sighed, looking down. ''Sometimes I think of it in terms of fear and at other times, almost as a welcome relief.''

I wasn't up to dealing with this new topic, and neither was she. It seemed years ago when I went to her house, not this morning. Amy had faced drunkenness, debt, divorce, disease. Surely death could wait one more day. We were not yet half way to Friday.

''Let's call it a day. Promise you will go home and get some sleep. And go easy on the booze. I want you here at nine in the morning, fully clothed and in your right mind.''

''You ask a great deal,'' she sighed.

''You have a great deal to give.''

I walked her to the door and watched her go to her car. As she drove away, she turned and waved. Amy looked like any other woman. Who would guess what she was going through? I wondered how many other normal looking people were going through similar darknesses, fighting for light.

I didn't want to think about it.

Faith for the Storm

7

Wednesday, 11:00 A.M.

Amy did not come at nine o'clock as expected but was coming at eleven. She had called to say she would be a couple of hours late and not to worry. No major problem. Just getting around slowly.

She sounded normal enough on the phone. She wasn't drunk, and hadn't been drinking. There was no need for a house call. And she promised to be at the office promptly at eleven. I had plenty to catch up on and hardly realized the two hours had passed.

When she arrived, her appearance concerned me. Amy was wearing the same dress as the day before, which in itself was no cause for alarm. But it was obvious she had not given much attention to her overall appearance. She was wearing sunglasses and did not bother to take them off. Her hair was partially beneath a scarf. She was smoking, the first time I had seen her with a cigarette, although I had noticed signs around the house the day before.

She was politely quiet. No small talk. No tears. The slight hint of levity she had conveyed on the phone was absent. Amy put out her cigarette and immediately lit another, using the wastebasket as an ashtray. I could not tell if she was looking at me. It seemed she was staring past me.

"I'm sorry about this morning. Hard time getting to sleep. Harder time getting up. Knew I had to come or you would . . . come to the house. Didn't want that again.

"Felt I should at least tell you this in person: I don't think we should continue this. I won't be coming back. I've wasted enough of your time."

"Don't you think I should be the judge of that?"

She made no effort to answer me, just smoked profusely, one cigarette after the other. It was the first time anyone had ever smoked in my office, a thought I wouldn't dare mention to her.

"May I ask what made you reach this decision?"

Again there was no immediate response. I was determined to wait her out, but soon wondered whether she was even aware I was in the room. I tried another track.

"Why didn't you tell me you were the wife of an ex-minister?"

"Because that was long ago and far, far away from where I am now." I expected her to ask where I got my information, but she reacted with total indifference.

"Has anything happened since yesterday that I should know about? You know me well enough by now to know I don't give up easily."

"Failure, that's all. Nothing new. Just the same. Nothing has changed. Nothing will. We both know my problems, and we both know there aren't any answers. My mother is dead. My marriage is finished . . . has been a long time. My children

don't need me. And shouldn't. My loneliness is
real. My health is poor. I've tried faith, but I can't
believe. Nothing changes. My drinking is obses-
sive, and I have no desire to stop. I don't care *how* I
will survive or *if* I survive. I'm not afraid of
failure—I'm surrounded by it. It is my present
condition. I accept it. I can't do anything about it.
Nor can anyone else.

"I am not being paranoid. I'm not pitying
myself. I am merely a victim of time and life. There
is no need going back through my problems one by
one. They all had a beginning, no doubt, but they
seem to have no end. I am physically and
emotionally exhausted. And nothing is going to
change."

"Amy, maybe everything you say is true. But do
you think you're the first, or the only person, who
has had to live with a problem which appeared to
have no solution?"

"I don't care what anyone else is going through.
That doesn't change my predicament. I'm without
faith in a world that I consider to be deprived of
God. You don't want to hear it. I don't like to say it.
But that's how it is."

"Amy, would you have faith if everything was
good in your life?"

No answer. I had misgivings about my reply, but
I didn't have many choices.

"Amy, one day Jesus was out in a boat with His
disciples. He had fallen asleep. A storm arose and
the men were afraid. They cried, "Master, save us
or we'll perish!" He awoke and calmed the storm.
Then He asked, "Where is your faith?"

"I think He was saying, 'Do you only have faith

in Me as long as the boat stays afloat? What would you do if the ship were to sink? Would you still have faith?'

"Amy, anyone can have faith while everything is going right. But there has to be a place for faith even when the ship is sinking."

I'm not getting anywhere. I wish she would take off those glasses.

"Amy, I honestly think you are a victim of our simplistic society. We are hopeless problem solvers. We reject the concept that there exists such a thing as a problem without a solution. We have been insulated from the unsolvable problems which confront other parts of the world. We have never experienced bombs being dropped on our homes. We have never lost a war.

"We have not suffered the failures of the world. We have had only pockets of hunger in a land of plenty while other nations have starved.

"We have hospitals and medicine for every imaginable illness, while common, curable diseases have wiped out millions throughout the earth.

"We are surrounded by comforts that we have taken for granted as necessities in our affluent society. The result is that we do not tolerate—even on an individual basis—the concept that there exists a problem without an answer. We develop a sense of shame over unsolvable situations. We even hide our sick, aged, and dying in closeted places. We deny dignity in death even to those we love by acting as though they really aren't going to die.

"Is it any wonder that you can't cope with the

idea of living with problems that cannot be solved? But people can learn to live with problems . . . do learn to live with failure . . . do learn to cope . . . to see things through.''

I had no idea whether she was even listening to me, much less comprehending. I felt at a total loss, groping . . . reaching.

''And you can, too, Amy. You must. I refuse to accept your resignation. Good goes bad. That's life. But bad can become good, or at least can be replaced with good. That's also life.''

Not immediately . . . but finally, she spoke.

''I do not see life as good or bad. To me it's meaningless. That's not being dramatic. I want no argument or advice. I feel separated . . . not just from my husband and family, but from life itself. My life is little more than raw nerve ends . . . an endless nightmare. It isn't a pretty picture, but it's *my* life.''

''But, Amy, you don't have . . . .''

She stood. ''Larry, I must be going. I do not feel well. I want to rest . . . to lie down and sleep. That's all I want.''

She reached out and shook my hand. ''I want to thank you for the time you have spent and for your interest.''

Her hand was moist and limp. She was through the door and gone before I could speak. It didn't matter, for I had no idea what to say.

She hadn't given me a chance. And yet, she had given me more chances than any person I had ever met. I had had all the answers but no solutions. Where was her faith? Where was my faith? Where was God?

It was still a long time to Friday.

One Ship More

8

Wednesday, 11:30 P.M.

The ringing of the phone awakened me. I did not know what time it was nor how long I had been asleep.

"Hello."

"Larry?"

"Yes."

"This is Amy."

"Amy, I have been worried sick about you all day."

"Larry, I wanted you to know I'm going to take my life."

I was wide awake. I heard what she had said but couldn't believe it—wouldn't believe it. I started to ask her to repeat it. Stupid! Cool, man, be cool.

"Where are you, Amy?" Call her name, keep calling her name. Ask her questions. Keep her talking. Cool.

"Amy? Where are you?"

"I'm at home. But I don't want you to come. I just wanted you to know. I wanted someone to know . . . and I didn't know who else to call."

"Amy, how do you plan to do it? How do you plan to take your life?"

"I don't know . I just know I am. Tonight. I must . . . don't you understand?"

Good. No plan. Good sign. Critical cases have plans. That's what the book says. Please be right.

"Amy, listen to me. I'm coming over."

"No, Larry. Please. It won't do any good . . . it will be too late. Please."

"Amy, I won't stop you. I promise. I swear, I will not lay a hand on you. I just want to be there."

"Goodbye, Larry. And thanks for everything."

The phone went dead. Frances was sitting apprehensively on the side of the bed, having heard my side of the conversation.

"Throw something on, honey. We've got to make tracks!"

All the lights were on inside as we pulled into Amy's driveway. I mean every light, including the one on the porch. I tried the door. It was open. I went in.

"Amy!" Not in the den, the kitchen. Maybe the bedroom.

"Amy!" The bathroom. Nowhere. The car. I ran outside. The car was gone.

"Oh, dear God, she's gone!"

"What did you say?" Frances thought I was speaking to her.

I got in the car.

"She has a fifteen minute start. Where would she go?"

"Do you think we should call the police?"

"No time. Think, honey, which way would you go?" I started down the street slowly.

"Larry, I think she would leave the neighborhood. A woman would worry about the neighbors, I think."

"Right." The freeway. I turned to the left. The

freeway was three blocks away.

"She wouldn't turn toward town." I turned onto the freeway away from town, still moving slowly. "You look on your side, I'll look on mine. She would either keep going a long way, in which case we have no chance, or she would take the first exit away from houses. Houses on the right, none on the left. Oh, God let us be right."

"Larry, I think we should call the police."

"She wouldn't use a gun, at least, I think not. Probably never fired a gun . . . probably afraid of guns." An all night service station on the right, I pulled in, and a man came out.

"Sir, did you see a woman in a dark brown Pontiac in the last fifteen minutes?"

"Sure did. Left here about five minutes ago. Didn't get gas. Just a coke out of the machine."

"Did she go into your restroom?"

"Nope. She would have had to ask for the key. Just got a coke and left."

"Did you notice which way she went?"

"Yep, headed east."

"Did she get back on the freeway?"

"Didn't notice. Just headed east."

I drove away. "Pills. She's got pills. That's why she bought the coke. She doesn't plan to go far." I stopped at the next street. Right and left—houses. I drove on. Next street, houses to the right, golf course to the left. Golf course! I turned left across the freeway. Drove a mile down the road.

"Larry, there's a car parked on the side of the road." It was Amy's car, and it looked empty. Pulling up behind it, I jumped out and walked to the car, afraid to look inside. Then I spotted the figure of a woman on the bridge ahead. *Has to be Amy. It is! No doubt about it.*

I walked briskly toward her. She was leaning on the rail looking down at the creek. She did not move. I stepped closer. Ten feet away. She looked at me. The coke was in her right hand and something—probably pills—was in the other.

"You promised not to stop me," she grumbled.

"I said I wouldn't touch you. But you know me. I talk. Well, that's all I'm going to do. I promise."

"It won't change anything."

I leaned on the bridge beside her and looked down into the water, unable to believe it had come to this. *Cool. Be cool.*

"I just want to know your reason. You've convinced me that you have nothing to live for. Now I want to know what you have to die for? What, Amy? Nothing we have discussed is enough to die for. There must be something you haven't told me." Talk. Get her to talk.

"Despair, Larry. We didn't mention despair. Total, absolute despair. It has become unbearable. At least it is less bearable to me than death."

"Why death, Amy? That's the absolute. All else is uncertain. Only death is absolute. Why death?"

I hoped that the word spoken often enough would repel her.

"Larry, I *want* to die."

"Amy, didn't anything we talked about—just one thing—apply to you?"

"Nothing applies to me unless I want it to. And I choose for nothing to apply to me because nothing appeals to me. Not one thing."

"Amy, coming to me for help must have

appealed to you or you wouldn't have called. Why this . . . now?''

"Larry, my motives for wanting to die are not important . . . because they are not even important to me.''

"If your reasons for wanting to die are not important to you, then why is dying important?'' Please, God, spare me stupidity!

"My death is only important because it is an alternative to the deep despair that keeps burying me as long as I live.''

Amy Wortham was no simpleton. She hadn't thought all this up tonight. She had gone over her lines God only knows how many times. At the moment, her intelligence was her worst enemy. I had to make it her friend. Reason was a limp weapon, but it was all that I had. If she left that bridge alive, she had to walk away on her own. She could have run when we arrived. Somehow, she wanted to be found. I had to believe that.

"I'm not afraid, Larry. But I know what Hemingway meant by 'The fear of life is far worse than the fear of death!' Because I'm not afraid to die, only to live. I remember reading from a book by Camus, who said, 'To lose life is a little thing but to see life dissipated is a terrible thing.' I see my life as being dissipated . . . and it is indeed terrible.''

"You're misquoting Camus, Amy. At least, you're taking him out of context. His entire book was against what you are considering.''

She doesn't want to do it. She's trying to talk herself into it. I know she doesn't want to do it. But that doesn't mean she won't. I had to gamble. I didn't know what else to do.

"Anyway, Amy, I don't believe you."

She turned and peered at me. "You don't believe I'm serious? You don't believe I honestly want to die?"

"No, I believe you about that, but you're being influenced now by your own arguments. I don't believe . . . the despair. I believe it's hope that's haunting you and I can prove it." *It's a risk. If she wants to hear me, she will. If not . . . .*

She did not take her eyes from me. *Those eyes! She's listening . . . listening with her eyes.*

"You say despair; I say hope, because that's where despair comes from. Listen to me. I'm going to give you a definition of your despair. It is the premature, arbitrary anticipation of the non-fulfillment of what you hoped for. Hear me out now. *Premature:* you are making a decision in advance of the 'not-yet'—I didn't say future. Hope is merely the not-yet. *Arbitrary:* no one is forcing this decision on you. Life isn't putting it upon you. Life is totally indifferent. You are arbitrarily making this decision. *Anticipation:* you not only believe in the non-fulfillment of what you hoped for—you are anxiously anticipating its non-fulfillment. All the bad has happened. But what you hoped for hasn't—not yet.

"So, what you call despair is your own cynical response to your deepest hopes. And don't tell me you have no hope regarding the not-yet. It was hope that brought you to my office. It was hope that made you call me tonight. And even now that hope is out there . . . just beyond your reach—but it is there."

She looked back toward the water below. Neither of us spoke. How I wanted to be able to look into her mind. A good five minutes went by. It seemed longer. *What is she thinking? Is she thinking? The longer the jury stays out . . . .*

"Larry, I . . . ," her voice was breaking, only slightly. She was not crying. ". . . don't want to die. I don't, but I must have something to cling to, don't you see? I've got to have something that is mine . . . not words . . . not your strength . . . something real that I know I can count on. And for the life of me, I have searched. And I can't find it. I just can't live without *something*."

My last gamble. I had to go for broke. If she would stay with me one more round, there was a chance. If not, I had nowhere else to go. The Lord had to want this or we were lost, for I didn't know how to put into words what had to be said. She wanted to let me help her, but she had too much integrity and sense to be bluffed.

"Make me a deal, Amy. If I can give you something you can count on, will you go home and meet me tomorrow?"

"Please, Larry, no more sermons. Not now. I'm not up to it."

"No sermon. I promise. A deal?"

She said nothing. I really hadn't expected her to, but she didn't stop me.

"*Time*, Amy. That's number one. You have time. You can count on it; right up to the moment you stop it, you have time. Time is real. Time is there. It is not a myth. You have time.

"And with time, you have *change*, Amy. That's number two. Time brings change. Nothing stays the same. Tomorrow will not be today. It may be better, it may be worse, but it will be different. Now the question is, do conditions always, without exception, change for the worse? Is there never such a thing as better days? Is all change always negative? The answer is no. Then it has to be true that something—anything—will change for you, for the better.

"And change for the good can be encouraged, assisted by *becoming*. That's number three. If Amy Wortham sits and passively wastes time, waiting for a change for the better, it will most likely not come. But if Amy Wortham seeks to *become* something better; if she is willing to strive toward becoming—toward influencing change in a positive way—if she will make a courageous commitment to the not-yet, then Amy Wortham just might—I say *might*—have found something she can count on.

"And, Amy, as sure as those stars are shining, I believe God will help you become what you hope for."

She was silent. I felt washed out. Hollow. There was nothing left. It hadn't come out like I wanted to say it. But I felt—sensed deeply—that she was listening.

"Amy, I'm going to tell you something I've never shared with anyone but Frances. I've never used this in a sermon. But one time I was low, very low . . . disappointed by people I trusted. Losing heart, I wanted to quit. Frances tried to get through to me but couldn't. Unable to shake my discouragement, I watched several years of planning and dreaming go down the drain. I was too emotionally exhausted to start over, yet the simplest thing reached me, because down inside I wanted to be helped, just as you do. A friend sent me a poem written by an eighty-four-year-old minister named Reverend Lindsay. It said,

If all my ships go out to sea;
And never come back to me:
If I must sit and watch each day,
An empty waste of waters grey.
Then I will fashion one ship more,
From bits of driftwood on the shore.
I'll build that ship with toil and pain
And send it out to sea again.

"Amy, let's try one ship more . . . together. I'll work night and day to help you build it. And we'll send it out to sea again—together."

I closed my eyes and prayed. There was not a word left. God alone knew the groanings coming from deep within me. I don't know what happened to time, how long we stood silently beside each other. A splash in the water below us shattered the stillness. A second splash quickly followed. I opened my eyes and saw the coke bottle slowly slip beneath the water.

"Take me home."

Nightmare

—— 9 ——

Thursday Morning

Who knows how a nightmare begins. There are those experiences so harrowing . . . so taxing . . . so emotionally exhausting that the horror is equally vivid and inescapable, asleep or awake.

The sessions that I had spent with Amy Wortham had drained me, mentally, emotionally, spiritually and physically. The severity of her problems had pulled from me everything I had to give—every bit of wisdom, knowledge, skill, experience, and compassion.

When I finally got to bed sometime in the early morning hours of Thursday, I realized full well that only the Spirit of God working through me could have succeeded in getting Amy off the bridge and safely home.

Safely? At least she was still alive. But I didn't have the slightest idea of how to deal with her tomorrow. No, tomorrow is already here. It's morning already, even though it's still dark. *Dear God, it's dark. Please Lord, send some light . . . even a tiny little glimmer to guide Amy back . . . .*

I don't remember going to sleep, but will never forget hearing the bells. Loud. Warning bells. I heard them, but couldn't wake up. Alarm bells. *Something is wrong. The world is spinning. Why can't I get awake to see what's happening? The bell keeps on ringing, ringing, ringing . . . .*

"There is a Paul Wortham on the phone. Says he is Amy Wortham's husband. I told him I would see if you were in."

Strangely enough, I had been thinking of Mr. Wortham that morning. It had occurred to me that the clue to reclaiming Amy for the Lord might rest with her husband. It must have been providential that he had come back to town at this strategic time in Amy's life.

"Larry Jones speaking."

"Reverend Jones, I am Paul Wortham, Amy's husband. I understand you have been seeing her."

"We've had several sessions together."

"Reverend Jones, Amy is dead. She cut her wrists. They think about five o'clock this morning. I arrived at the house from out of town about eight. When I found her, she was dead. She left a note addressed to you. I read it; she requested that you conduct her funeral. I was wondering if you could meet me at the funeral home after lunch. I'll give you the note, and we can discuss the arrangements. We would like to have the services on Saturday. Can we meet at one o'clock this afternoon?"

"Yes, I'll be there."

I put the phone in its place. The buzzer for my intercom sounded again. Ignoring it, I stared at the chair across from my desk. Again the buzzer sounded . . . then again.

The door opened and my secretary leaned in. "Is your phone working? I've been trying to reach you. The call you placed to Dallas is ready."

Her words went unanswered. My eyes continued their fixation on the chair. She stepped out, closing the door quietly.

I stood, my eyes scanning the room: the magazine left open on the sofa in the corner, the cigarette butts still in the wastebasket from the day before, the number on the note pad. The name!

I walked slowly out of my office, down the hall, out the back door to my car. Slipped into the driver's seat, started the motor, and moved slowly out into the traffic. The freeway soon appeared before me. I turned east. Took an exit. Left on the road to the golf course. Some fifty yards before the bridge, I pulled to the side of the road. Turned off the motor. My hands on the wheel moved closer together, crossed, my arms resting one on top of the other. I lowered my brow against my arms, and closed my eyes.

My shoulders began to shake.

* * * * * * * * * * * * * * * * *

A few minutes past one I pulled into the back lot of the Michner Funeral Home as I had done many times when coming to attend or preach a funeral. John Michner was a long-time friend. His father, who founded the business, had died earlier in the year. John was my age. We had played basketball in college together. I had called ahead to let him know that Amy Wortham was special to me.

When I entered John's office, he was sitting with a man I presumed to be Paul Wortham. Both men stood.

"I'm Larry Jones," I smiled, extending my hand.

"This is Paul Wortham, Larry. I thought you knew each other."

"No, I knew his wife but not him." I referred to Paul as though he were not present, looking toward John as I spoke. Wortham was only slightly taller than I, not as heavy, with light hair and shaded glasses.

"This is for you," Paul offered soberly, handing me a folded sheet of paper. It was the note that Amy had left.

"Thank you." I took the note and placed it in my inside coat pocket, not wanting to read it in front of an audience, much less Paul Wortham. "John, could I speak with you privately for a moment? Excuse me, Paul, but I have another matter to discuss with him before we talk. It won't take five minutes."

I stepped into the hall. John followed. When we were through the double doors at the end of the hall, I turned to him.

"I want to see her, John."

"Now? Larry, we haven't finished with her yet. I mean they haven't brought us what she's going to wear. They haven't even selected the coffin."

"Where is she?"

John turned and walked toward the embalming room. I followed, my heart pounding, hating what I was about to do, yet wanting to—having to. I must know. Must be sure.

Amy was lying on a white table in the center of the room. She was wearing a plain white robe. Her hands folded across her chest, she looked like an angel. Eyes closed. Almost smiling. Peaceful.

John left, closing the door behind him. I went closer, stood beside her, placed my hand on hers. I watched her face, waited for her to speak . . .

waited for her cold hand to grow warm . . . waited for her to say, "Take me home," as she had last night.

I had driven her car while Frances followed. We did not speak during the brief ride to her house. She had fallen asleep, her head against the window. I was glad. She must have been exhausted.

Frances had gone with her into the house and stayed until Amy was in bed. The last time I saw her she was walking into the house, Frances by her side. She never looked back.

I took the note from my pocket.

Dear Larry,

It has been only an hour since you and Frances left, and already I am awake again.

I want to thank you and Frances for your kindness to me. And thank you for caring and for everything you told me. For a few moments tonight, I felt so strong. But I knew it was your strength, Larry, not mine. Once before, I lived on another person's strength. I thought we were immortal and that love was eternal. Then one day the love and strength were both removed, leaving me only my mortality.

I cannot live again in another person's strength, even for one more day.

I love God, Larry, and pray that He will forgive me for what I am doing and that you will forgive me too.

Would you please do me one last favor and conduct my funeral? And will you stay with me until they have put me safely in the ground and covered me? I just don't want to be alone.

Please tell my children that I love them.
                    Amy

Tears flooded my eyes, and the grief that I felt inside tumbled with them down my cheeks.

"Oh, Amy, why did you do this? Didn't you know it wasn't my strength but the Lord's? And He never would have forsaken you. Oh, Amy, why couldn't you just have trusted me until you were able once again to trust the Lord?"

John's voice slipped through the opening door. "Larry, Mr. Wortham is waiting."

The three of us talked briefly in the conference room adjoining John's office. The service would be at 10:00 a.m. Saturday morning in the chapel. A private service was planned for the family at the graveside. When we had finished and were about to leave, I asked Paul to stay behind for a moment.

We remained seated in the conference room as John left. I was almost afraid of my feelings for the man across from me. I wanted to say, "If you had been here, she would not have died." But I didn't.

"Paul, I know this is not an easy time. Perhaps I should explain my relationship with your wife these past few days. Since our first conversation by phone last Sunday evening, I met with Amy in counseling sessions at least twice a day, sometimes three. Despite our best efforts together, she became increasingly desperate."

Paul's reply seemed cold . . . blunt. "Amy has had her good and bad times for some time now. On occasions, she expressed little more than mild indifference, at other times deep depression."

"Then you judged her condition to be at least

one for concern and at most, serious."

"I am not a doctor, Reverend Jones, and not qualified to make critical professional judgments."

Nor was I, was the implication I drew from his statement.

"Am I correct in assuming she was referring to you in her note?"

"I'm sure Amy explained to you that we have not been close of late. I'm also certain it was difficult in your sessions to disassociate yourself from my ministerial background and to view our relationship merely as husband and wife."

"Amy did not mention your having been a minister. She only referred to your marital relationship as something she feared losing."

"Reverend Jones," he sighed, never taking his eyes from mine, "you hold me responsible for Amy's death, don't you?"

"I'm not God, Paul. And I'm certainly not in a position to make that kind of judgment. I am interested in knowing what damaged her faith, which I'm sure once was very real to her. At times, she spoke out of an intensely deep theological background about her feelings of meaninglessness. That kind of training is not easy to come by, and not easy to shake. But there's no doubt about it—it was shaken."

Paul nodded, face serious and thoughtful. "Amy and I entered the religious scene early, both of us obsessed with success—which we had. I played the lead and Amy the supporting role. I was the first to drift from faith as the center of my universe, leaving her with no lead to support and unable to play the lead adequately herself.

"From there, the problem was compounded by our drift from each other. Amy was left with neither a vertical nor a horizontal frame of reference."

"And your own personal pilgrimage was more valuable to you than your home or her life." It did not come as a question as I had hoped, but as a statement which subconsciously I had intended.

Paul Wortham did not respond as expected. He leaned toward the conference table and spoke more softly, yet still firmly.

"Larry, in the present setting you are God and I am the devil. I understand your position. I have been, far too many times, in the position of dealing with people on the brink. I have battled fiercely for their soul as well as their life as I'm sure you did with Amy. And it matters not if you win or lose, *until you lose*. And the loss is almost unbearable, for the stakes are always beyond any fixed value.

"In Amy's case, I am the wayfaring husband who might have saved his wife from death. I was not in the heat of the battle. And I am far from proud of my position.

"I will tell you this, and you can take it or leave it. I would do anything to get Amy back, although I do not believe that we would have, or even should have, stayed together. There was too much pretense, too little honesty, and not enough love.

"But I must also say this: I will not accept responsibility for Amy's death or her life, nor would I for any other than my own. We both know there is no meaning in life itself. It is up to each person to create that meaning by what he chooses to believe, by whom he chooses to love, and by how he chooses to act.

"You have chosen to act in faith. I have chosen to act apart from faith. Amy was somewhere in between. But it was her choice because it was her life.

"Her mode of dying does not discount her faith—not for me. On the one hand, she had exhausted her emotional resources. On the other, there is the probability that for the believer often more hope exists in death than in life."

"Paul, I'm glad we talked," I responded quietly after an awkward moment of silence. "I did not want to see you. I resented, and still do, any person, word or deed which helped bring Amy down. She was such a beautiful person. Her life was so worth living. She had so much to give. Her death is a senseless waste.

"In all honesty, Paul, at times like this I feel like hanging up my diploma as a minister. I simply cannot deal with the absurdity of death."

"Who can, Larry? And I do understand any ill feelings you have toward me. In fact, I am comforted by them, for they stem from a genuine love for one who was dearer to me than you might imagine. And I'd like you to know this, although I don't feel I owe it to you to say it: I am neither an atheist nor an agnostic, simply a man in search of himself. If there is a God, He has concealed Himself from me and the world in which I live. Perhaps that is so I will remain solely responsible for my life. And I do accept responsibility for that."

There was nothing more for us to say. I had no sermon for Paul Wortham, and he wasn't asking for one. But I still had one more sermon for Amy. One I did not relish.

We shook hands and parted. We would see each other one more time at the funeral on Saturday.

Saturday. But no Friday.

The Vision

—————10—————

Saturday, 10:00 A.M.

The chapel was packed with beautiful faces and charming people. It was truly an elite gathering. Amy had been an officer in a women's service club, a garden club, a tennis club, and her college sorority. I marveled at how little I had known of Amy . . . and yet how much. Somehow I had viewed her as being alone in the world, for that is how I found her, and that is how I left her.

Her children were also remarkably attractive. One of the two girls, Connie, was a look-alike to Amy. The son, Paul Jr., tall and tanned from the golf circuit, was the image of what his father must have been like in earlier days.

The front of the chapel was banked with flowers. They surrounded the pale pink casket, lined the walls, and even extended into the corridor.

Amy looked very young. There was a bow at her neck, a flower in her hair. Looking at her from my position on the platform, I thought of her breast surgery. How much it had meant then. How little it mattered now.

I was not over the loss of Amy. She had been my first major defeat in fourteen years. This was my initial firsthand experience with suicide. Although it had become the fourth major cause of death in our nation, I did not concern myself for the other sixty thousand plus victims—only for the girl

before me, for she was *that* until the last day: a
middle-aged little girl. Perhaps it was the dreams
and hopes of youth that she would not relinquish
which killed her. Amy never grew old. She just
gave up.

A quartet finished a second hymn. Dr. Garnish
of the First Baptist Church read a Bible passage
and led in prayer.

I stepped to the podium and opened my Bible.
Not having a sermon that seemed appropriate, I
scanned the faces before me and just shared the
thoughts and feelings that had been welling up
inside me.

"When I first met Amy Wortham a week ago
tomorrow, she made a very simple request of me. I
had no doubt that I could fulfill it. She asked me to
help her make it to Friday. At first, I did not
fathom the significance of Friday, much less
believe for a moment that it would never come.

"As a minister, I have always placed the
greatest significance on Monday. For me, it was
the day for beginning again. It became a weekly
resurrection. It held the possibilities of fresh
starts, new ventures, and renewed efforts.

"But I was fortunate, for I viewed the future in
bright rainbow colors of hope-filled prospects. I
was on top of life, looking forward with renewed
vigor and vitality. That is how I viewed life . . .
from Monday.

"Soon I learned I was out of step with our
society. For most other people, it seemed, the key
day was not Monday, but Friday. A week was not
to be exalted for its beginning but its end, not for
its promises and potential, but for its finality—its

fruition.

"At first, I took this new insight as lightly as I learned it. In my younger years, I had been a working man looking forward to three things: whiskey, women, and Friday.

"I smiled when I learned of a new chain of restaurants across the land called T.G.I.F.— 'Thank God It's Friday.' The name was somehow symbolic of a new national pastime—everyone trying to reach Friday.

"Then last Sunday evening the concept took a deeper meaning, for the cry which came to me was in earnest. The request was intensely serious: 'Help me make it to Friday.'

"To me, it seemed all but absurd. I had made it to every Friday in my existence, usually without effort and almost always with bright anticipation.

"But the cry which came to me was from one who did not think she could make it to Friday. And indeed, she did not.

"And thus Amy Wortham died. Her death once again has defined for us the total devastation of alienation. For Amy Wortham was not merely alone, but alienated from every person and every living thing—including you who sit in this room. You contributed, each of you, to her condition, if not by what you did, by what you failed to do, not merely for Amy—but against alienation.

"Do you not see how this very gathering today is a mockery to Amy's plight? Many of you are here today not because you loved Amy or even really knew her, but because you were a comrade with her in a group—a club, a society of you who chose to find strength in numbers—in standing together.

Why, then, did Amy die alone in your midst? "Obviously, it is not a requirement for membership in your group to really reach each other beneath the veneer of surface relationships. You never actually know each other in your mutual desperations, fears, and needs. This is sad, for it *is* a requirement for membership in life that we love each other—or we die.

"So I hold you responsible, each of you, for the death of Amy. You are guilty for not reaching out—for not caring—for not sharing—for not being. 'Don't blame me,' you say, 'I didn't know.' And that is the source of your greatest guilt, for ignorance is no excuse for apathy and indifference. What *do* you know about those closest to you? Your husband or wife, child or parent? What do you know about the person sitting this very moment to your right—or left? What do you care?

"It should give this gathering today cause for reflection that your member . . . your relative . . . your sister felt so alone, so deserted, so out of touch, out of step, out of favor, so out of friends that she memorized the phone number of a stranger on television.

"And so . . . Amy and I met. What does it say about desperation for a woman of intelligence, friends, and accomplishment to place a personal call to an anonymous number? Amy's call was one of many, for we pay people to sit by phones and answer calls for help. But for Amy, it was a singular act—one call. It was the only call she would make about one life—her life.

"The nature of the call also speaks volumes. She did not seek ultimate answers to long range problems. Her sights, hopes, plans, fears, were shortening faster than we imagained. She only wanted to know how to make it—how to stay afloat—how to survive with dignity, integrity, and meaning for just one week!

"I accept responsibility most of all for the death of Amy Wortham. Your sins were only ignorance and indifference. Because of her call, I knew. And having been brought into her fight for meaning, purpose and value, I cared.

"And I tried. God knows I gave it my best! I said all I knew, did all I could. Why? Let me make a confession. Amy Wortham as a single individual was not that important to me—not at first. Quickly, however, she became more than one woman. She became every woman . . . every person. In the past I had tried to help other people in a feeble, halfhearted way, because they had not pressed me as Amy did. They had not defined the scope of their dilemma with as much intensity.

"She became more. She became those who never sought help but struggled on silently, lost in the masses. She represented those we pass each day on the streets, or sit across from each day, or lie beside each night. She became you . . . and you . . . and you . . . .

"I am here today because it was Amy Wortham's parting request. I certainly would not seek such an assignment. I have no idea what she wanted me to say to you, her friends and loved ones. It may be she wanted me to ask you something.

"What if Amy Wortham had placed the call to you? What if she had said to you, 'Help me make it to Friday?' And what if you had spent this last week with her instead of me? If you had been confronted with her sorrow, loneliness, guilt, anxiety, fear, doubt and despair, what would you have offered her? What would you have laid before her and said, 'This, Amy, and this and this is what makes life worth living?'

"You may say, 'It is no longer important.' But it is! It is more important than ever. Amy is gone, but you are still here. And the problems that Amy faced are universal. If you had nothing to say to her, how can you think you are prepared to face the times of darkness which may be ahead for you?

"Amy Wortham brought me into her battle too late in the game. I console myself with that even if it is only partially true—or not true at all. If it is true, I dare say that Amy didn't know. She could not have known how late it was or she would have never called. She did not pick the time of her departure. It picked her. I am convinced that for quite some time Amy had been taking one step forward and two steps back in her struggle with life. She could not know, as no one can, how long or far she would go until her back would be to the precipice—that backward step that would take her over the brink.

"Nor can you know, as you sit here today, at what stage you are . . . what darkness will be yours to go through . . . what cup will be yours to drink. We do not relish the thought of preparing ourselves to live life on any other plane than the one which is not ours—immortality. We do live as immortals planning, preparing, hoping, right up to the day, as Amy said, 'Our mortality overtakes us.'

"It is not too late for you — only for Amy. It is not too late for you to care . . . to reach out to those around you . . . to find the courage to remain on the brink . . . to learn to hold faith and despair in delicate balance. Amy thought she had to make a choice between the two. There is no such choice. There is no faith without despair, no despair without faith. The courage to be demands them both . . . the courage to accept acceptance . . . to remain under the burden . . . to learn to be happy . . . to hold fast to faith while battling with the pain of despair.

"I do not doubt Amy's faith, although she did. She did not trust faith . . . or hope . . . or the future. She could not trust anybody — her friends, family, or most of all, herself. But they were all there, though she could no longer see them . . . touch them . . . feel them. They were there, waiting . . . to the end.

"If a man dies, shall he live again?

"Yes — and if he does — he can live again and again. That, in hindsight, is what I did not say to Amy. She had indeed died to past dreams and hopes. If only she could have believed, she could live again to new hopes, new dreams.

"I cannot leave you with a new insight which will allow us to say Amy Wortham's death is worth her life.

"I can only assure you that life's brink awaits you as it did Amy. And when that time comes for you, as surely it will, you will have two choices: take your life . . . blow your brains out . . . take your pills . . . cut your wrists; or find the courage to live again . . . and again . . . and again.''

There was nothing left to say. I closed my Bible and sat down. Two attendands lowered the lid on the casket and began moving the coffin on its rollers toward the rear door. Eight pallbearers, friends of Paul, carried the casket to a waiting limousine.

The crowd filed out of the chapel and waited outside, encircling the limousine holding Amy. They waited while Paul and the children entered a second car. This would be their last tribute, since it had been announced that only the family would go to the graveside.

Choosing to drive to the cemetery in my own car, accompanied by Frances, I parked behind the three black Cadillac limousines and followed the men carrying the casket to the grave. When they had returned to their car, the family members were escorted by an attendant to four chairs beneath a small tent beside the grave.

When they were seated, I stepped to the head of the coffin, which was resting on straps for the final lowering process. The sun was high in the sky — not a single cloud could be seen. A large oak tree formed an umbrella over the tent, as well as the grave. The site overlooked the rest of the cemetery, a slight hillside looking down on a valley of trees and the carefully landscaped gardens in full bloom. A faint breeze carried the sounds of distant traffic, hidden from view.

I opened my Bible and began reading from its last book.

And one of the elders answered, saying unto me, These are they which came out of great tribulation, and have washed their robes, and made them white in the blood of the Lamb.

Therefore are they before the throne of God, and serve Him day and night in His temple: and He that sitteth on the throne shall dwell among them.

They shall hunger no more, neither thirst any more; neither shall the sun light on them, nor any heat.

For the Lamb which is in the midst of the throne shall feed them, and shall lead them unto living fountains of waters: and God shall wipe away all tears from their eyes.

I closed the Bible, shut my eyes, and began to pray:

"Dear Lord, we stand at this place convinced that Amy Wortham is not here but has already risen far beyond the heights of our imagination and at this moment is with You.

"May these loved ones carry with them the fondest memories of this woman. And may they also leave with a new high resolve to live with the knowledge that they will also someday stand before You. In Jesus' name. Amen."

I made my way toward the individuals in the four chairs. They had stood and were waiting for the guidance of the attendant. One of the daughters carried a rose and laid it on the coffin. A second attendant pressed a button which began lowering the coffin into the ground. The other daughter, Connie, approached me.

"Reverend Jones, did Mother speak of us

children when she talked with you?"

"Yes, she did, Connie. She spoke of you a great deal. She loved you very much."

It seemed there was more that Connie wanted to say, but she turned away to watch the coffin disappearing into the ground.

Paul Jr., who had been standing beside his Father, walked over to me.

"Sir, do you really believe my mother is in Heaven? I mean with the way she died and all?" He was much taller than I realized. He continued, not waiting for an answer.

"I love my Mother and Father very much. I never tried to mix in their problems. But I want you to know that I am a member of the church because she took me and encouraged me. I thought you should know that."

"Paul, your mother was so deeply troubled in these past days that she did her best not to let me see her better side. But I was wise enough to see it anyway. That is part of Amy Wortham, the only part, I care to remember. I would hope you will do the same."

He shook my hand. It was a strong hand, a firm grip. He left to join his father and sisters who were making their way down the hill to the car.

I sat in one of the four chairs and watched as three men with shovels filled the grave from the mound of dirt. I heard the cars pulling away behind me. The workmen were speaking to each other in Spanish, laughing as they continued with their work.

Two of the attendants returned and began carrying some of the flowers to a van which had been driven close to the grave site. Soon the attendants stood to the side, speaking so low that I could not hear their conversation. Finally, they left. Moments later, the three workmen also left, and I was alone.

I was in no hurry. It was a beautiful day.

* * * * * * * * * * * * * * * * * *

I don't know what awakened me. I suddenly opened my eyes and realized it was morning. *But what morning?* I looked around the familiar surroundings of my bedroom . . . light slipping around the edges of the window shade, my clothes from the night before were draped over the back of the chair. Frances was already up—no wonder, the bedside clock said 8:45. *I must have overslept. Why do I feel so sad inside . . . so heavy . . . as if part of me had died? Died? Wait a minute! There's something strange here . . . .*

Pulling on a robe, I went out to the kitchen looking for Frances. She was gone. A note on the table read simply, "Call you later." She had placed it where I'd be sure to see it, along with the morning newspaper.

I slipped the rubber band off the paper and unfolded it to read the headlines. But it was not the lead story that caught my attention. It was a word in small type at the top of the page . . . a word in the date. I read it—closed my eyes, then opened the paper and read that word again.

Thursday . . . .

Thursday! But what about the lost Friday and that awful, heart-rending Saturday and . . . .

Thursday. But that means last night was . . . O

thank God! There's still another chance, another opportunity, another day. I've got to get moving. Must get to the office and check on Amy.

There's still one day 'til Friday.

A New Beginning

11

Thursday, 10:00 A.M.

I did not suggest that Frances do it. This was her own idea. It was her day to take the neighborhood carpool for school. On these mornings, when she drives, I usually meet her returning, when I am on my way to the office.

But Frances had left with the kids before I was up. Once the depression of my nightmarish dream had been shaken, my mind began racing again, filled with thoughts of Amy and the experience of the preceeding night. I remember wondering where Frances had gone as I drove to the office.

She also had been thinking of Amy. At times, I failed to give her proper credit for her awareness, her perception, and tenacity. This morning was one of those times. Frances had driven directly from school to Amy's house. Finding her still in bed, but awake, Frances had made coffee while Amy showered and dressed. Frances called me to say that Amy would be in to see me about ten o'clock. Although little conversation had passed between them, Amy was in a fair frame of mind.

Frances and Amy were going to meet later for lunch. Amy's response to the invitation was far from a spirited commitment, but they had mutually agreed that the prospect of getting out had merit.

I had been pondering the best approach to make things as easy as possible for her under the circumstances, when my telephone intercom announced Amy's arrival.

She entered the office and sat in her normal place. Her appearance revealed none of the pressure under which she had been. Wearing a bright yellow dress, with white shoes and purse, she was putting up a good front, I had to admit. But her first words set the record straight.

"I feel extremely embarrassed, very humiliated, and generally frustrated. I think I might have made it here without Frances' help this morning, but I'm glad I didn't have to try." Without waiting for my response, she continued. "I'm at a complete loss to understand either my feelings or my actions. I'm not certain I would have followed through, even if the two of you had not come last night.

"But that's the humiliating part—that I was even considering it." She looked away. "It isn't a comforting self-image to know that you were actually *considering* taking your own life. All of the reasons I had for not finding meaning to my life were real—not imagined—and still are. The prospects for the future are still dim. But I did not really want to end my life, and still don't. I don't have the courage to die—or any reason to live. I can't even succeed in taking my own life. Last night was an exercise in futility."

"Not futility, Amy. Intermission. That's how I choose to look at it. Maybe we all needed the pause. Maybe the flirting with death was good for us. We now know more clearly what our aim must be. Life is the thesis before us. Death is the antithesis . . . the contradiction to life. It is our job now to find a synthesis, to find meaning and value and possibilities in the midst of your life and death situation—which is no more or less than the task every human being faces.''

"Larry, I'm so mixed up; I can't even stick to the role I'm playing at any given moment. I say that I'm not sure I would have gone through with it last night, but I'm not sure that I wouldn't. I mean, I was afraid—afraid I would, afraid I wouldn't. I wanted to and I didn't want to.

"Then, when you and Frances came, you talked and I listened. God! I think I remember every word you said. But in the midst of the tragic, I involved myself in the mundane. I began to think how rude it would be to do it and to inconvenience you and Frances. Can you see what I'm saying? Of all the reasons you were offering for my living, I was opting for petty, surface reasons of appearance. How unladylike to kill one's self in the presence of friends.''

"That's why we were there.''

"But you weren't there when I got back home. You can't always be there.''

"True. But you must remember that I was there by invitation. You *did* call.''

"Then you think that I will never do it . . . take my life?''

"No, quite the opposite. Most people who went as far as you did last night will go that far again unless things change for the better. Next time you will probably pick a more secluded time and place . . . maybe even wait until after the pills have been taken to call.''

"You don't offer a very positive prospect."

"Let's just say, I take what happened last night very seriously, and I think you do, too."

She looked down. "If you want to know what I think, I think I'm a fake. I feel . . . like a real sham."

"I'm not sure you were faking as much as you believe. Surely, Amy, you don't think that you are under obligation to prove that you can kill yourself."

"No, just to prove that I'm not a fake. I hate phony people. I despise pretense. But I did what I felt. I went to the brink because I felt like I had to. And I didn't follow through because I no longer felt like it. Dear God, it's a horrible thing to be a slave to my feelings when they are so ambivalent. They not only change from day to day, but from moment to moment. How can one live like this?"

"Amy, we are making a full circle. You can't divorce yourself from your feelings, but you can work at redirecting them. Your feelings are the result of what you've been thinking. The longer you dwell on something, the stronger the feeling will be which follows from it."

"Then it's back to thinking nice thoughts and hoping the badman won't return," she sighed.

"Presuppositions, Amy. That's what we must carve out for you. There must be a basis for thought, a basis for belief, for plans, for preferences. You're not suffering from mixed emotions but random thinking. And that comes from a lack of structure to your outlook toward yourself and life."

She looked up at me. There was no way to read

anything good or bad into her expression.

"Then we are back to Monday, aren't we? Because I am about to repeat my opening question to you — where do we begin?"

"No, not back to Monday, Amy. We're light years away. We know a thousand things which aren't the answer. We also know each other better . . . enough so that we can both put aside pretense and try to get to the heart of the matter."

I looked at my watch. There was not enough time to go any further. I stood.

"Amy Wortham, you look ravishing. Keep reminding yourself of that . . . and you two have a good lunch. Then, be back here at two o'clock, at which time I'm going to tell you the most important thing you'll ever hear. I have skirted it, but never said it to you. Now I am going to say it. It is not only the most important thing I have to say, but the most important thing you need to hear."

She stopped at the door.

"Larry, was this lunch a put-up job? Be honest. I wouldn't mind either way."

"Amy, I didn't tell Frances to ask you to lunch. I didn't even ask her to call you this morning. I don't know her reasons for doing either, nor do I care, nor should you. Enjoy yourself, Amy. Relax. It's a beautiful Thursday, and both of you are beautiful women. You can do a lot for each other. Just keep putting one foot in front of the other, Amy, try it. One step at a time." The intercom . . . that would be Frances.

"We would be happy to have you join us," her voice sang. It was not an invitation.

"Heavens no! I would be bored to death.

Besides, someone has to stay here and keep the sky from falling.''

I watched as two women went out the front door.

Moment of Discovery

———— 12 ————

Thursday, 12:00 Noon

They sat in the garden area of the restaurant under a canopy lined with hanging baskets. Their talk throughout the meal had been predominantly about their children.

Finally the conversation came to men, and Amy discussed her relationship with Paul openly and perhaps objectively for the first time. It became evident to Amy that I had shared little with Frances of our conversations.

"I didn't intend for us to talk about my problems, but I did want to thank you for allowing yourself to be dragged into all this."

Frances did not offer a response.

"I could have died when I learned you had been sitting in the car for hours the other morning. And then last night."

Again Amy's words were met with silence.

"Frances, I don't know which way to go, and I'm frightened. I feel as if I should be locked up somewhere. I shouldn't be out on the streets acting normal when I feel cut up into little pieces on the inside. What right do I have to be sitting here as though everything is roses? I thought I could pull it off, but I'm not up to it. Do you think I could be losing my mind?''

Frances looked at her, smiling. "Amy, I want whatever is best for you. Please know that. But Larry is the counselor, and I think we'd better leave all this between you and him.''

Amy put on a pair of sunglasses, started to take a cigarette from her purse, then put it back.

"Please forgive me. You're right. It's terrible to be so introspective. I can't seem to keep my wits about me. I haven't always been this way.''

Frances called for the check. "Amy, it's been good to get to know you better. I don't want to be short with our time, but I must be at the doctor at 1:30.''

"Oh? Is it something you can tell me about?''

"I only wish I could—I mean I wish I knew. It's been a long, drawn out affair . . . actually into the years now. I've had surgery eight times, but we can't seem to get a handle on it. I get tired very easily . . . no strength at all. There seems to be no end to it.''

"Frances, I had no idea.''

"Think nothing of it. I've left the matter entirely in the Lord's hands. I do the best I can and look to Him for the rest. I don't believe in carrying burdens that I'm not strong enough to bear alone. Many people take their troubles to the Lord but don't leave them with Him. They pick them up and keep carrying them. That isn't trust.''

She looked directly at Amy, smiling. "I know it may sound a bit pious, but I do trust the Lord, Amy. And it works for me. I will not allow my days to be marred, worrying about things beyond my control.''

She did not take her eyes from Amy.

''And it might surprise you to know that Larry also has been ill for quite some time. For almost a year now he has had dizzy spells, trouble with his balance, severe headaches, and very little strength. Several months ago he didn't get out of bed for weeks. And Larry has been a picture of health—literally a health freak most of his life.''

''Strange,'' Amy mused, marking on her napkin with a spoon, ''I would have thought you two were problem free.''

''No one is, Amy. That's the only reason that I shared these things with you. Perhaps I shouldn't. Larry would have told you if he had thought it best. But Amy, people just don't exist who are free from private concerns.''

''And you think I've been selfish to think only of myself—which is true!''

''Not at all. Quite the contrary. You have no choice but to stay with your life until you can get a direction. But you can't expect to go from empty to full overnight—if ever. The Bible says, 'in all these things,' not despite them, 'we are more than conquerors.' Happiness, or well-being, does not come from losing one's problems, but in learning how to deal with them.

''There,'' taking her purse in hand, ''that is the end of my sermon. And please don't breathe a word of this conversation to my husband, or he won't let us go out alone again,'' Frances laughed.

Leaving the restaurant, they stopped to compliment the new manager and comment on the decor.

God Believes in You

—————13—————

Thursday, 2:00 P.M.

Amy entered the office a few minutes early, but did not take a seat. She walked to the window and stood looking out.

"Larry, I don't feel very well. I think last night is catching up with me. I don't know that I'm up to a heavy session. I just want to sleep . . . and forget."

"Sit down, Amy. Lie down if you like. Just listen to me. If what I have to say puts you to sleep, I won't mind. You don't have to say a word. Just listen."

She took the chair across from the desk. I noticed she was looking past me again. She had been able to make a good showing this morning, but was running out of steam. Did fatigue produce depression or was her depression creating fatigue? She could not have slept more than four hours last night. Should I let her get some rest?

"Would you like to go home and rest awhile?"

She leaned her head against the back of the chair, closing her eyes.

"It doesn't matter."

"Amy, it's your life that we're talking about. If it's not worth fooling with to you, I don't know how you can expect it to be important to anyone else.''

Without changing her position, she opened her eyes and stared at me. At first a look of surprise crossed her face, then a more stoical expression.

''What was it you wanted to tell me that was so important?''

''That God believes in you.''

She closed her eyes again.

''We've already been over this, and I've told you repeatedly: I'm not even sure I believe in God, at least not enough to make a difference.''

''That's not the first step—your belief in God. The first step is for you to realize that regardless of your present concern for Him, He believes in you.''

''Well, knowing the facts, He certainly isn't choosy about whom He believes in,'' she caustically replied.

''But that's the whole point. He knows you thoroughly . . . better than anyone else . . . better than you know yourself.''

''He knows all the bad and still believes in me?'' She was remaining convincingly unconvinced.

''Right. But He also knows all the good—not merely the good you have done, but the good of which you are capable. He knows your potential and what you could become. And it's all a matter of climate.''

''Climate?'' She straightened up in the chair to get into a more relaxed position.

''Climate.'' I continued, ''Do you know why we don't have as many palm trees here as there are . . . say in Miami? Climate. That's all. The winds constantly scatter the same tropical seeds throughout the land and the only reason they don't take root is climate.''

"What are you saying?''

"There is, at this very moment, as much potential for happiness and peace of mind in Amy Wortham as there is in any other human being. The seeds of possible contentment are sown indiscriminately throughout humanity. But you have lived so long now in a problem-oriented climate—much of it self-induced—that it has rendered your whole life counterproductive.

"And if He can ever get you out of the hazardous, foggy, dense climate in which you have surrounded yourself, God knows there is more contentment and happiness for Amy Wortham than you ever dreamed possible.''

"I'm sure God is all that interested in me, seeing the mess I've made of my life.''

"You are correct. He is interested in you because He loves you with a perfect love—a kind of love that we know little about . . . it is unconditional. Our love for each other on a human level is almost always conditional. We begin by telling children that if they aren't good we won't love them. Later in life, we don't offer our love to another person until he or she meets our conditions. They must make us love them.

"But God gives us His love in the midst of our failures and mistakes. His love inspires us. The pages of the New Testament are filled with examples of God loving unlovable people and, in the process, changing them for good.

"You might say Jesus Christ made a habit of surrounding Himself with misfits—a crooked tax

collector, prostitutes, the proud, the ill-tempered
. . . you name it. But He offered them His love,
His trust, His care.

"You can almost write the biography of Jesus
Christ while He was on the earth by using two
words: 'try again!' Wherever He found people who
were down, for whatever reasons, He did not
condemn them or write them off. He loved them,
and said, 'try again.'

"And that's what He offers you now, Amy. His
love . . . His faith in you . . . His concern. And He
wants you to try again."

"Well, I don't know how." She defiantly sat up.
"Can't you understand I've been through all that?
I've *heard* all those words, and I've *said* all those
words. They didn't work for me. And I won't be a
phony—not for you, not for anyone!"

"Maybe you had the words, but not the music,
Amy. Maybe it was not your faith but Paul's . . . or
your faith in Paul's faith. Genuine faith works,
Amy, but if it didn't work for you, it either wasn't
your faith . . . or it wasn't faith at all. Either way,
it was a fake. I'm not asking you to be another
phony. I'm asking you to be real, to stand on your
own!"

She closed her eyes again, her private defense.

"Why did I have to come to a preacher? I
jumped out of the frying pan into the fire, wouldn't
you say?"

I strode to the window and replied, "I may be a
preacher, but I'm not just trying to save your soul.
I could have given you three points and a prayer
Monday morning and had you out of here in
nothing flat. It's your *life* I'm wanting to see saved,

and you know it! But I'm *not* going to water down the truth, Amy . . . not for you or for anyone *else.*"

"You know, Larry, you're a fighter. That helps me more than any of the words you've said. You didn't tell me Frances was ill or that you had been having trouble also."

I moved to the side of the desk and sat down.

"Amy, I grew up in athletics. I went to college on a basketball scholarship. In sports you learn very quickly to live with pain. You get injuries early in your career, but you never really get over them. You learn not to gripe and not to quit."

"Do you think I'm a quitter?"

"Far from it, or you wouldn't still be here . . . would you? You just happen not to like preachers, people, truth, hope, love, and faith. Other than that, you are perfectly normal."

"I think that's overstating the case, but I'll accept it for now. Have we reached an impasse?"

"Until dinner. You are coming to our house. You can see how the other half lives."

"Babysitting—is that another one of your talents? Am I not to be trusted alone?" she taunted.

"Not for the duration. My contract expires Friday. I plan to see personally that you make it, so I'll see you at seven o'clock sharp."

How to Handle Doubt

—14—

Thursday, 7:00 P.M.

As I cooked the steaks in the backyard, Frances and Amy talked while preparing the rest of the meal. The kids had been sent away for the evening. This was not a social event, and the three of us knew it. Frances had suggested the change of scenery.

The idea was good. I would be leaving town for three weeks the next afternoon. Frances would remain behind. If the two women could be friends, I welcomed it.

I had not begun the week planning to spend it entirely with Amy. Two out of every three weeks, sometimes three, were spent on the road. My time at home was normally spent taping television and radio programs, which left little time for personal counseling.

Amy's case had almost become a crusade for me. Probably for the first time in my ministry, I had become aware of the quick, easy answers I had given to others. This thought had come back repeatedly to me during the week.

I had given a full week to Amy Wortham, but all I could think of now was that there wasn't enough time. I was running out of time, things to say, and generally growing weary. Amy couldn't and shouldn't be pressed. I recalled a game in college when we were trying to make up a twenty-point deficit in the last half. We cut the lead to seven points with two minutes to go, but we were physically running out of steam. You can only call on your resources for so long and then they falter.

Although she probably hadn't detected all this in me, I had the feeling that this was happening to Amy. In the past few days she had undergone the most consistent mental, physical, and emotional drain of her life.

The strain also was evident with Frances, as she had been as much a part of the experience as I. Her reserves were short and she had not complained, but the spark was not there.

After dinner, Frances insisted on cleaning up. Amy and I went into the den, taking our coffee with us. She had worn jeans, by mutual decision of the women. During dinner, Amy had spoken how her secret sin had been doubt, which she had harbored through the years, even while she was a minister's wife. Not having any plan of attack or prepared speech, I pursued the subject of her doubt. I had come to realize how insignificant the immediate subject was in our conversations. All roads usually led to the same core—how to get a grip on life. I also had become more comfortable with dialogue, an exercise we ministers never seem to trust. We are so used to telling people what to do.

"Tell me about your secret sin. Was it God's existence you doubted?"

"Oh, Larry, it was more than that. I doubted everything from as far back as I can remember. I'm sure a lot of people accept things without question.

Not me. I was a regular 'doubting Amy' . . . about anything and everything. I was born with an above average skeptical spirit. I couldn't help it. If there was a question on my mind and no one had an answer for it, I simply couldn't stand it. Women are accused of living by instinct, but that wasn't true for me. My spirit was laid in concrete. It 'instinctively' demanded fact and logic, it asked questions, listened, waited, and questioned again.''

''There's nothing wrong with honest doubt, Amy. Understand, I said honest. But a lot of doubt is not honest. Often it is simply a cloak to hide our cynicism. People often doubt the existence of God merely because they do not want a Master in their lives. Others doubt there is such a thing as absolute morality because they do not want to be good.

''But there is much honest doubt which should be encouraged. History, for instance, is literally patched together by doubt. There could be no progress without it. Galileo doubted the earth stood still, Copernicus doubted the earth was the center of the universe, Columbus doubted it was flat, Newton doubted that nature was erratic, and Einstein doubted the earth was fixed.

''The interesting thing is that all these men were basically religious, but they did not give up their faith when they began to doubt. However, all of these men were looked upon as outcasts by the organized religionists of their day. Some suffered all but excommunication from the church because of their doubts. And yet, you and I understand our world better today because these men doubted.

"Therefore, the question is not whether a person doubts. Every person does. The human personality is divided into two parts—part faith, part doubt. There are certain things you and I disbelieve. Certain things we accept on faith. Our natures are structured that way. And strangely enough, as we broaden our knowledge, we also lengthen our margin of uncertainty. The more that we know, the more we realize that there is more we do not know."

"But surely, Larry, there are people who have no doubts about things."

"I have never met that person—who can say, 'I don't have a question; there are no shadowy places in my life; it's all figured out! I know everything I need to know.'

"That person simply doesn't exist. The question is not whether we doubt; rather, what should we do with our doubts? No matter how small they are. Whether they involve some seemingly insignificant factor in daily living, or whether they include something far more serious relating to the very meaning of life. What should a person do with doubts?"

Amy waited, "Are you asking me, sincerely?"

"Of course. I'm interested to know how you think a person should deal with doubt."

"Well, let's see, you can read books on the subject. Or talk with people who are authorities in that area. Or you can reason the matter out for yourself."

"Those are all good as second, third, and fourth alternatives. But the first thing a person should do is take it to God. Lay your questions before Him and ask His help.''

She smiled, almost condescendingly. ''Larry, is life genuinely that simple for you? Do you have only one answer for all questions? This may be the best for you, but you aren't everyone. What if a person's doubts center around God? What if she does not believe in God, or that God, if He exists, either cares or can do anything to alter things as they are? Does one turn to prayer and say, 'God, I don't believe in You — help me?' ''

''Right! That's exactly what I'm saying. Earlier in my pilgrimage of faith, I was greatly encouraged by the conversation of a famous professor from a prominent Eastern school. He was a genius, but steeped in skepticism. He was considered dangerous to those of faith because he was so genteel. He was not the kind of man to stand in the classroom and lecture against principles of faith in God. He was too polite for that.

''But when someone raised a question about religious faith, he had a way of smiling as though he understood there were those still naive enough to believe. It was obvious to all there was no place for belief in God in his life.

''One day a girl came up after class and said, 'Professor, I have a serious problem.'

''He said, 'Tell me about it. I'll do my best to help.'

''She said, 'My problem is that my faith in God is very real to me. But I also respect your intelligence above any human being I know. I can't reconcile my faith in God with your lack of faith in God.'

''Then she said this: 'Sir, if I could only be sure

you had actually sought after God and not found Him — and I don't mean in books, but sought after God's presence in your life directed from God and not found Him — I think I could gain the courage to give up my own faith.'

"Then she asked a direct question, 'Sir, have you ever prayed?' Caught by the question, he replied that he had never prayed in his life.

"She said, 'Then would you do me a favor? And please understand, I am not trying to gain faith for you, but settle a problem in my own life. This is how I found God, through prayer. But I realize I do not have the intelligence that you have. I'm going to ask you to pray for just a few days. Just sincerely ask God's help in your life. And after you try to seek God's help, if He doesn't help you, I will give up my faith.'

"Dr. Horace Bushnell was stunned. He thought a moment, and told her that he would do it. As quickly as he consented, he added, 'But young lady, since I do not believe in God, how will I address my prayers?'

"She asked, 'Don't you believe in anything?'

"He said, 'Yes, I believe there is a principle of right in the world.'

"She said, 'Then instead of saying, "Dear God," why don't you pray to the principle of right? I think if there is a God, He will know you are trying to address Him.'

"For three days Horace Bushnell did not meet his classes. On the fourth day he came to class and announced, 'Before I begin my lecture, I would like to relate an experience I have had.' He described his conversation with the student.

"Then he explained, 'For the past three days, I have been alone in my study with one book—the New Testament. I followed a pattern which I thought would be fair. I determined to read through the New Testament, and to read very carefully the Gospel of John. Periodically, I would put aside my reading and say this prayer:

'Dear God, if there is a God, give me light if there is light to give; and if I receive light, I will do my best to follow it until the day I die.'

"Then he said, 'I want to say in the hearing of this young lady that today I not only believe in God, but count myself a follower of the Lord Jesus Christ.' "

For a time we sat in silence. Frances had entered the room and was sitting alone on the sofa.

"Larry, are you telling me that all of the questions that I have . . . all the problems in my life will be solved if I get alone in a room a few days and just pray?"

"No, that is not what I am saying. Not at all. You may come away with more questions than you have now. But if you dare to sincerely seek God's help, honestly place your life at His disposal, and earnestly seek His guidance—you will come away from that experience unburdened and with a new spirit. You will discover that the walls of your mind have widened. You have a new confidence. Your new, brave heart will enable you to have courage to return to the search . . . determined not to give up.

"Was it honestly that clear cut and simple for you, Larry?"

"Frankly, it was just the opposite. I was already a young ministerial student, armed with faith, when I began to encounter the waves of doubt. I watched a couple of fellow ministerial students turn back, because there seemed to be too many unanswerable questions.

"I made up my mind that before I threw in the towel, I would do something positive. Everybody was doubting any ultimate meaning of life, including God. This seemed too easy of an alternative, so I decided to question those who were doubting God.

"Amy, please forgive me if I made it sound simple, or easy. I went through hell in my fight to overcome the doubts concerning the meaning of existence. And I was fighting giants—some of the greatest minds of all the ages.

"I stormed Kaffka's *Castle* trying to get in, frantically fled through Sartre's *No Exit* trying to get out, and lived through Camus' *Plague* trying just to survive with integrity. I heard the dying minister screaming, 'I must believe everything or deny everything.' I wept over Lagerkvist's *Barabbas* in his futile efforts to find answers, followed Conrad to the very center of his *Heart of Darkness*, struggled with Freud to hold on to a heavenly father, and attended the funeral of Bernano's *Country Priest*.

"You could never know the pain it was for me, Amy. My life was in the balance. It was no mild intellectual search that I was enduring. I had to find a place where I could stand against the storms in my soul. Everywhere I turned there were questions . . . questions without answers.

"Wounded and exhausted, I patiently and persistently explored the depths of my own heart.

And I almost cried aloud to find within my own experience, questions of my own, for which none of these men had answers. One supreme question they could not answer.

"When I was a boy, I remember going to church and hearing the preacher talk about sin, and I knew he was talking about me. And when I heard him speak of judgment, I knew that I was responsible for my life.

"Then he talked about the love of God. He began to describe this person, Jesus Christ, who lived on the earth. He told of Jesus coming to earth to show God's love, His dying to prove that God would forgive me, and how, through His resurrection, I could walk in newness of life.

"I began to identify with the sinner, the love of God, and the need for purpose and direction for my life. For you see, all this time I was like a boat without an anchor . . . drifting . . . . Going nowhere.

"I found myself burdened with a heavy sense of guilt. This was years before I had ever heard of Horace Bushnell, but I found myself praying a prayer similar to his.

"Dear God, if there is a God, give me light. Let me know of Jesus Christ. Let Him breathe new life into my life. And if He will forgive me and help me, and give me direction, I will do my best to follow Him.

"Amy, I'm not saying it happened in a flash from above but, during the following days, something began to happen inside of me. When I came to a complete commitment, I began to release myself into the hands of God and receive

the knowledge of Jesus Christ into my life
personally, then the burden of guilt began to
vanish. For the first time, I knew where I was
going. I would get up in the morning and feel that
life was worth living.

"No, my questions weren't all answered, and
still aren't. But that isn't important. I can live with
what I don't know as long as I have faith in what I
do know happened to me. Augustine said, 'I
believe that I might understand.' It is never the
other way around. You can never understand in
order to believe."

I wanted to say, "And that can happen to you,
Amy," but it wouldn't come out.

The room filled with silence and minutes
dragged by without a word.

"Your strength, Larry. We are back to your
strength, not mine. I am not as strong as some and
I never have been. My doubts are probably not the
same as yours. My faith, or lack of it, certainly
isn't the same. I'm far more concerned about faith
in myself than anyone or anything else.

"By now you must understand that I wasn't
searching when I came to you. I was running . . .
hiding . . . holding on. That's why I mentioned
Friday. I just wanted to get through a few more
days without losing my . . . everything. I only
found you by accident . . . just desperate . . .
that's all."

"Amy, it doesn't matter why or what brought us
together. What matters is that we are here. You
asked me to help you make it to Friday, which is
only hours away. I have a gift for you. I have
waited to share it with you . . . until tomorrow.

You may not want it, but it's yours, if you will receive it.''

We agreed to meet at 9:00 the next morning.

The Priceless Gift

15

Friday, 9:00 A.M.

When Amy arrived, she brought with her a red rose in a tall, thin glass vase. Placing it on the corner of the desk, she sat in her regular place.

"Am I supposed to guess its significance?"

"You mentioned a gift, and I don't like to be caught short . . . that's part of it, but most of all, it's for Friday. We made it, didn't we? It didn't mean that much when I first said it, but having lived it . . . this week—I cannot describe to you how precious this day is to me."

"When you first mentioned it, I had no doubts about our making it. I guess we both underestimated the significance of your words."

"And now for my gift. Don't offer a woman something, then hold her in suspense too long!" Her eyes twinkled with expectation.

"I hope you won't be disappointed. It could have been a ploy to make sure you came. I'm not above it."

I handed a blue leather Bible across the desk. She opened it and read the inscription: "To Amy, from Larry and Frances—Friday, May 26, 1978."

"In all honesty, the Bible was an afterthought.

The gift I spoke about last night relates to something else.''

"I'll always cherish this, Larry. What you wrote in it is more meaningful to me than what the other men had to say within its pages, for that is mine alone.''

I leaned back in my chair and took my own Bible in hand.

"You've made a better man out of me, Amy. You've caused me to read this book much more than I normally do. After you left last night, I reread a story from the book of Mark where Jesus told a man that if he would believe, his son would be healed. The man replied, 'Lord, I believe, help my unbelief.' The man was saying, 'I'll believe the best I can, but I must be honest, I don't believe a lot of things. If I'm ever going to make it, You are going to have to help me overcome my unbelief.' ''

"The application, if intended for me, is accepted,'' Amy nodded. On almost every subject I am one part belief and two parts unbelief—which to me is no faith at all.''

I replied, "Last night, you referred to the desperation which prompted your calling me. I read the book of Mark in the light of your statement and it's amazing to see the various motivations which led people to a personal confrontation with Jesus. Most of the people He helped had little faith when they approached Him, or no faith at all. In fact, many of them didn't even know who He was when they came . . . which wasn't important . . . the main thing is that they came. Faith, for them, almost always came later.''

She fingered the Bible in her lap nervously.

"I don't follow you."

"It tells us that God does not expect one to come with a full, untarnished, all-knowing faith. He does not expect one to come saying, 'Okay, God, I now have answered all the questions. I understand all the things which concerned me, know exactly who You are, what You are, what is expected of me, and what I'm supposed to do. Therefore, I bring You my mature faith and lay it at Your feet.'

"It tells us, rather, that all God asks for is an empty shell—where you would put faith, understanding, and knowledge, if you had it.

"God then takes your empty shell and puts the faith in for you—not all at once—but in time."

"But, Larry, I have always looked upon faith as something one does—'have faith in this or that,' 'place your faith in Him.' "

"No, Amy. That's all wrong. *Faith is a gift from God*—not something you conjure up."

I walked around the desk, sat beside her, and opened her new Bible to the book of Ephesians.

"Let me show you. 'For by grace are you saved through faith; and that . . . (faith) . . . not of yourselves; it is the gift of God!'

"That's the gift I was talking about, Amy. Faith. You can't muster up faith on your own, as if you were baking a cake, with faith being the ingredient you are to provide. You make the choice to give God a chance, and He puts faith into your life."

A frown crossed her face. I was missing the mark.

"Well, He hasn't put many ingredients in my cake!"

"You haven't given him much chance. Now stay

with me a minute, Amy, and listen carefully;
please try not to misunderstand. We do not have a
great deal of choice over what we believe. If you
keep exposing yourself to certain ideologies, certain
values, certain environments, you soon become
engrossed in them . . . they affect your beliefs.

"In your case, Amy, you have been away from
religious values, away from church, and away from
the Bible. It's no wonder your faith is weak."

I could sense that she was on the defensive. I
stood and walked to my swivel chair.

"The fact is, you have helped me in this area,
Amy. Because of you, I realize I have possibly been
imposing too much on people in my crusades. At
the invitation, I have been asking people to come
forward and confess that they believe.

"I'm going to begin encouraging people to come
and say, 'I don't believe,' because that's where
most people are. I'll invite them to come and say, 'I
have an emptiness within, if I could only believe,
faith could fill the void.' I've been asking people to
come saying, 'I can believe.' I'm going to start
asking them to come saying, 'I can't! As long as a
life is still open—God can and will supply the
faith.'"

The most encouraging thing about Amy on this
day was that she was no longer passive. Although
her questions remained, the air of fatalism—of
futility—was missing.

"Larry, with my background, I'm embarrassed
to admit this is a problem to me, but I do not
understand faith. Is that ridiculous? Definitions
fail me here. Does it mean 'to buck up?' Does it
mean, as the queen told Alice, 'to take a deep

breath and try again?' The words, belief . . . trust . . . faith are all hollow and meaningless to me.''

"Amy, when David Livingston went to Africa, he thought he understood what faith was and that others also understood. He discovered that the Africans had no word in their dialect for it. Objects were easy to define but concepts, such as faith, were bewildering.

"One day as he was sitting at his desk in his tent, his servant returned from a hunting trip. In sheer exhaustion, the servant walked into the tent, took the pack from his back, and fell onto the cot. Livingston turned to him and asked, 'What did you just do?' The servant, in his own dialect, described the act of falling exhausted onto the cot. Livingston said, 'This is faith.'

"This is faith, Amy—*to fall in God's direction* and let Him catch you and help you. Life doesn't have many easy answers and doesn't automatically fall into place. There are many alternatives and we are called upon to make choices . . . before we know the full impact of our decisions. Investments have to be made before we know whether they will pay off.

"This is all God asks of us in the matter of faith. He wants us to come to Him, not critically or defensively, but openly, saying, 'If there is help, I want it. If there is understanding, I will accept it.' This is all that He asks us to do.''

"Larry, I understand choices when they are clear cut—between good and bad, right and wrong, better and best. But for the life of me, I see none of these choices in what you have offered me. On one hand, I see my problems, bleak as they are, and on the other I see faith plus a dark, uncertain future. Is there something I'm missing?''

For the first time she was pulling with me.

''Amy, I'm afraid that's how it is. Soren Kierkegaard, the Danish philosopher, used this analogy to define our choice. He described a man sitting in a boat just off a small island. The boat was sinking, and crocodiles were coming from the distance. The man was close enough and had the time to swim to shore.

''But on the island, he could hear the roar of a mountain lion. Here were his alternatives: he could stay with the boat and sink, in which case he would be eaten by the crocodiles—or he could swim to the island where he would face the possibility of being eaten by the lion. His choices were: to stay with no hope, or swim toward little hope. Two bad alternatives: one offered virtually no chance, the other only a slightly greater prospect for survival. So he chose to swim—not toward safety—not toward certainty—but toward chance. Kierkegaard called this the 'leap of faith.' As the men of old said, 'Why sit we here until we die?'

''When you swim toward faith, Amy, you can't be sure what the future holds. You don't know that you will find the answers to your deepest needs and desires. You only have what the present holds. If you find that lacking, why not take the chance of faith, and swim toward what you don't know? It's as simple as, 'Lord, I believe; help my unbelief.' ''

She had almost become a part of the scenery. I had learned to read every look—away, down—the closing of her eyes. Her silence.

''Larry, your words last night and this morning

have come to me from a distant, but well-known shore. I wanted to hear you say them because they conveyed your concern and sincerity, but I honestly can't say whether I relished them or resented them." Quickly she went on, not seeming to trust an interruption in what she wanted to say.

"Surely you realize your task has not been to convert me. I sat for ten years and heard those words about faith, trust, and the like, from one of the most eloquent ministers of our day. I know you have some knowledge of my past. You must know that the religious portion of my life has been seriously damaged. Paul and I both played the religious game. We were not blasphemous or overtly deceptive, but neither were we sincere. Through the years, faith in myself, in God, in others, and in right was as easily lost, as it had been gained."

"But you are no different from others, Amy. The inner life of a person of faith is always a turbulant struggle, and your strength is something that most constantly be renewed.

"I knew I was taking you over old ground by talking about conversion and commitment, but there was no other way. Your false starts and setbacks in your spiritual and emotional pilgrimage do not make God's Word and guidance in your life void.

"I want much more than this for you. I long for you to capture . . . or regain—whatever—to lay hold on the priceless value of your own right to selfhood and authenticity.

"Amy, you have a right to commit yourself to your own well-being—free to *be* yourself and to love yourself in your day-to-day experiences of life.

"This is all you have. You must seek after the knowledge and acceptance of yourself as a person of worth. Don't you see? That's all you would have lost had you taken your life. Your mother would still have been dead. Your husband would have continued his own life. Your children would have survived your loss. Your friends would have hardly missed you . . . and then not for very long.

"All that would have been lost was Amy Wortham. You are your own legacy. You are you and you will never be anyone else. The commitment of faith must be to yourself. God wants abundant life for Amy Wortham, but you are the only one who can lay claim to your life. You had the power to take it but only you can say 'yes' to your life. And you must begin with yourself.

"In order to lay claim to your own life, you must free yourself from others, so that you will be able to love them and relate to them better . . . as the individual you are.

"Freeing yourself from the past will give you better understanding so that you can enjoy the past.

"And you must release yourself from your life up to this very moment, in order to live again. You do not live one life—no one does. You live many lives. And, as an animal sheds its winter coat, a human being sheds one life to begin another.

"I want you to live again, Amy. Have the courage to consider yourself dead to your other lives, not that you cease to be, but rather that you rebuild your inner self. Make new plans and dreams—not theoretical goals in the dim, distant future, but practical, down-to-earth steps to take you one step at a time into the new life.

"This is your gift to yourself—your acknowledgment that Amy Wortham deserves to live again."

I stood and walked to the window, my back to Amy.

"You are in a unique position but you must take advantage of it. Your life is before you . . . open to all the possibilities you can conceive. Consider everything up to this point as dead, as part of another life—and a new life awaits you."

I turned facing her.

"You have no time for remorse, guilt, or fear. Your new life will begin the moment you accept it as new. It's yours if you will lay claim to it. Life worth living is not without pain and struggle, but it's there, and it's yours. And any day—even Friday—is a good day to begin a new life."

She had not spoken for some time. Whether she had listened I did not know.

"What time does your plane leave?"

"Frances is to pick me up at noon. I leave at 1:00."

"Then I would like to be there to see you off. You will be away three weeks?"

"Yes. Poor planning on my part. I need more time at home."

She stood. "I'll see you at the airport."

The Promise

———16———

Friday, 12:30 P.M.

I had checked my baggage and was at the gate, when Amy appeared from nowhere.

"I know you have little time, but before you leave, I wanted to tell you where I am."

They were calling for the boarding of the plane.

"I have decided to get a job. Don't laugh. People do still hire the handicapped. I may volunteer for service at the hospital to work with the aged. I honestly enjoy being around older people. I realize I resented my mother because she died so soon in life.

"The marriage is in Paul's hands. If he wants to try again, I will. If not, I refuse to equate divorce with death.

"I'm going to postpone my feelings about my operation. For now, I am alive. That's a fact . . . as you would say.

"I'm going to start attending church—not for all the lofty reasons you would desire. I'm not there yet. But I want the stimulation. Above all else, Larry, you stimulated me and made me think again.

"I'm going to visit my kids, act like a mother, and let them think of ways to entertain me. I won't feel sorry for myself and wonder why they don't call. I raised them. They deserve me. Mainly, I want the excuse to move around.

"Larry, I know you wanted more. But at least I have faith in me. I think I like me. Where it goes from here, I don't know . . . but at least I care. That's a start."

Last call. I took her hand and kissed her cheek.

"And you can go with this: When you return, I'll still be here. And I'll be three weeks old."

I kissed Frances and ran. I turned at the steps of the plane, but the women had walked away.

I started up the steps. Three weeks is a long time. Three crusades in a row. Lord, help *me* make it to Friday.

"I am myself again . . . the machinery has started up again . . . broken is the spell that bewitched me. No one is there . . . no one questions . . . demands. The cup of intoxication is handed back to me again. Long live the flight of thought . . . Long live danger in the service of an idea . . . Long live the hardship of combat . . . Long live the dance in the whirl of the infinite . . . Long live the wave that hurls me above the stars."

Repetition — Soren Kierkegaard

For further information concerning Larry Jones' ministry, please write: Larry Jones, Box 36, Oklahoma City, Oklahoma 73101.